BUILDING SOCIAL CAPITAL

Self help in a twenty-first century welfare state

Mai Wann

The Joseph Rowntree Foundation has supported this project as part of its programme of research and innovative development projects, which it hopes will be of value to policy makers and practitioners. The facts presented and views expressed in this report, however, are those of the authors and not necessarily those of the Foundation.

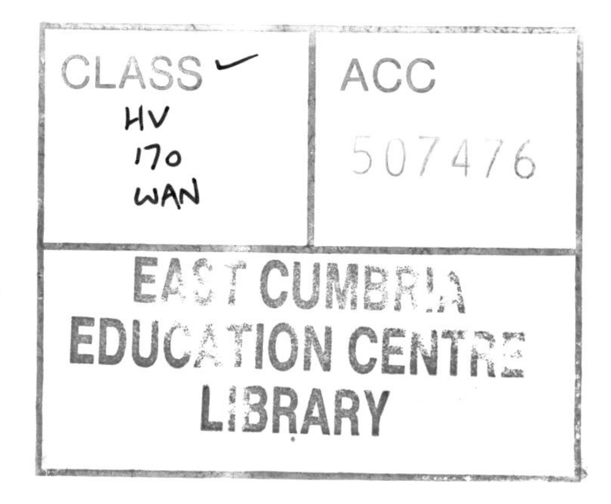

CONTENTS

THE AUTHOR

Mai Wann is an experienced practitioner and leading analyst in the field of self help and mutual aid. She set up the Self Help Centre at the National Council for Voluntary Organisations in 1986 and co-ordinated its work until 1990. She has been a consultant and trainer for self help support activities, both nationally and internationally, and has worked with women's and ethnic minority groups at a local and regional level. She now specialises in the evaluation of voluntary sector projects.

AUTHOR'S ACKNOWLEDGEMENTS

We are grateful to the Joseph Rowntree Foundation for funding this study. Judy Wilson of the Nottingham Self Help Team has been a generous and highly valued consultant on this project. My warmest thanks to her and to Katy Ferguson, whose research laid the foundations for the study. I am grateful to all those members of self help groups and support workers who shared their knowledge and experience, to those who attended the IPPR seminar on Self Help and Public Policy, which helped us to formulate our ideas, and to Nicholas Deakin for his advice. Finally, many thanks to Anna Coote, Director of IPPR's Social Policy Programme, for devising the project, editing the report and drafting the final chapter.

SUMMARY

Self help and mutual aid activities have expanded rapidly over the last two decades, not only in Britain, but in most Western democracies. There is broad agreement that they can bring considerable benefits to individuals and communities. What part should they play in a 21st century welfare state?

What is self help?

Self help has been inspired by ideas such as those of Samuel Smiles who advocated individual self-improvement, as well as those of Russian anarchist Peter Kropotkin, who favoured co-operative endeavour. More recently it has been influenced by the ideals of community development and the women's movement. It has taken root in eastern and central Europe, a symbol of renewal for civil society in the post-communist era. Contrary to the conventions of charities, voluntarism or post-war welfare states, self help is about personal responsibility and interdependence as well as direct, local action. Its ethos is empowering and enabling rather than protective, prescriptive or philanthropic.

Self help groups are formed by people who share a common problem or condition who get together for mutual support and to find new ways of coping. They are run along informal lines and there is an assumption of equality between members. Their core activities are to provide emotional support, information, advice and practical help, to recruit members, to carry out publicity and education, fundraising and (for some) campaigning.

What can self help achieve?

Self help can bring benefits to individuals in a great many ways. Two of the most common are ending personal isolation and providing practical help. It can also effect wider changes. Self help groups can help to shift power from providers to users of public services, to influence public policy by bringing lay people's views to the attention of policy makers, to challenge established values and traditional roles and to promote research.

Self help has limitations; it is not the answer to everyone's problems. Not everyone wants to share their problems, or to listen to other people's; some worry that self help groups are stigmatising and can isolate their members from the rest of society. Group activities can give rise to conflict among members; domineering or 'difficult' individuals can hijack the proceedings. People who are ill, overtired, geographically isolated and poor may be less able than others to contribute to and benefit from a self help group. It scores high on creativity and diversity, and low on equity and consistency.

The scope of self help

Self help can be seen as part of a spectrum of activities, linking and overlapping with self care, group therapy, befriending, advocacy, community development, lay participation in local decision-making and campaigning. Self help groups fall into six major categories: physical illness, disability, mental health, carers' groups, addiction and social issues. Self help activities vary from one category to another as they are adapted to meet particular needs and conditions.

Groups tend to go through similar stages of development, which have been dubbed 'forming, storming, norming and performing'. They have different requirements at different times in their life-cycle. Some groups are linked with national organisations which liaise with local groups, provide networking opportunities and services for them, and campaign on their behalf. Some form partnerships with statutory agencies to provide services in a locality.

Problems and possibilities

Key issues which represent a challenge to the development of self help groups include rural environments, relationships with professionals, organising in ethnic minority communities, questions of leadership, evaluation and consultation, and the availability of resources. These must be explored and understood by policy-makers.

Support for self help

While autonomy is the hallmark of self help groups, their autonomy as well as their effectiveness may depend on receiving support from outside. Existing support is either local and general or national and specialist. Support activities include compiling and disseminating information about local self help groups and national umbrella organisations, liaising with professionals in health and social care, producing information on how to form and run a group, and (sometimes) acting as facilitators for local groups.

The Self Help Alliance was a pilot scheme run by the Department of Health in 1986 which set up 18 projects to support self help in different parts of the country; the funding was for three years only and none of the projects has survived intact. Other examples of self help support are the Nottingham Self Help Team, the Manchester Self Help Resource Centre (which closed in 1993), the Doncaster Self Help Forum, and national organisations such as Body Positive, the Alzheimer's Disease Society, the Endometriosis Society and CancerLink. The Self Help Centre at the National Council for Voluntary Organisations acts as an umbrella for self help support organisations and workers.

Self help in Europe and North America

In Germany, Belgium and Denmark, self help groups are developing with support agencies, similar to those in Britain. There are also groups, though less commonly, in southern Europe, for example in Barcelona, Spain. In Eastern Europe, notably Hungary, self help groups have mushroomed after the collapse of communism, but they tend to be rather different in character, more outward-looking and focused on practical ways of meeting needs. International meetings of self help participants and support workers have been held in Frankfurt (1991), Canada (1992) and Denmark (1993).

In the United States, self help groups developed rapidly in the 1970s and 1980s, as well as clearinghouses to support them. Computer networks are widely used to link groups and members.

Summary of recommendations

- Public policy should acknowledge the scope and scale of self help activities and the contribution they can make, directly and indirectly, to the health and well-being of the population, and to the vitality of civil society.

- A remodelled welfare system for the 21st century should recognise self help as a core activity. That implies understanding its strengths and limitations, organising support systems around it, and changing the ethos as well as some of the practices of the statutory services.

- The aim should be to create the conditions for all kinds of self help activity to flourish in all kinds of community; to spread opportunities for self help widely and as evenly as possible.

- To this end, public funds should be invested in local organisations which offer support to self help groups. Funding would be relatively modest but should be on a continuing basis, to be distributed by the Department of Health and possibly administered through Joint Consultative Committees. It is envisaged that one support organisation would be set up in each locality, and that a range of local organisations could be invited to apply for the grant.

- Self help support should be encouraged to develop gradually and experimentally, using a range of models to suit different conditions.

- One or more national umbrella organisations for self help support should be publicly funded to provide training, networking opportunities, and liaison with self help overseas, as well as with policy makers and opinion formers.

- Self help groups cannot be subject to quality control, but self help support organisations should be monitored and evaluated.

- Longitudinal research should be commissioned to explore the effects of self help on individuals and communities.

- Public investment in self help support should be kept under review, taking account of the evaluation of support organisations and long-term research findings.

- Criteria for monitoring performance of self help support should be developed in consultation with self help groups, professionals in health and social care and others with relevant experience.

- The central role of self help should be reflected in training programmes for professionals and local government officials. If self help is to flourish at the heart of a 21st century welfare state, then the 'experts' must respect the autonomy and capabilities of self help groups.

- A new strategy for the voluntary sector should be developed alongside a strategy for self help. This must recognise the essential differences between self help groups and most voluntary organisations, and seek to build a constructive relationship between the two.

INTRODUCTION

Across Europe and North America,[1] the last two decades have witnessed a vast expansion in the activities of groups devoted to self help and mutual aid. This development has important political implications. It runs counter to the conventions of post-war welfarism as well as to the older traditions of charity and voluntarism. Self help and mutual aid stress personal responsibility and interdependence, as well as direct, local action. They present an ethos which is empowering and enabling rather than protective, prescriptive or philanthropic. They challenge the power and expertise of professional groups, especially in the field of health. All this comes at a time when the search is on for new strategies to tackle social problems and meet individual needs.

There is broad agreement that self-help and mutual aid activities can be beneficial. The consensus has developed among participants as well as among community workers and professionals in health and social care - from observation and experience, since there has been no systematic research. Such activities are thought to bring benefits not only to the individuals who take part in groups, but also to communities and sectors of society who experience change as a result of the groups' endeavours.

The development has occurred without any significant intervention from political parties or governments. Groups spring to life and expire spontaneously and randomly; together, they have an anarchic quality which defies external regulation. For a range of reasons, they are viewed with both favour and suspicion on the left and right of the political spectrum. They have few powerful champions, perhaps because they lack any clear political identity (except that they are antithetical to centralised and *dirigiste* regimes: the collapse of communism led to a sudden surge of self help and mutual aid activity in Eastern Europe). Should governments continue to turn a blind eye, or is there a case for a new public policy for self-help and mutual aid? Should these activities continue to be regarded as marginal, or should they be brought into the mainstream as policy makers attempt to reinvent the welfare state for the 21st century?

In order to address these questions it is necessary to consider what is meant by self help and mutual aid, what the groups do, and their strengths and limitations. This account begins with a description of the range of functions they cover and their common characteristics. It describes their particular activities in relation to specific groups, ranging from people with cancer and people with learning difficulties, to drug addicts and survivors of sexual abuse. It considers common patterns of development among self help groups and goes on to identify key issues relevant to public policy and current models for supporting groups and activities. It examines experiences from other European countries and from the United States. Finally, it offers conclusions and policy recommendations.

Self help without mutual aid, as a purely private activity, is not relevant to this discussion. Mutual aid implies helping oneself as well as - and through - helping others. However, 'self help' is used throughout this discussion to denote a combination of both activities, simply because it is the more familiar term.

1. WHAT IS SELF HELP?

To understand what is meant by self help, we consider its ideological roots, the characteristics shared by most self help groups and their core activities.

Sources of inspiration

The concepts of self help and mutual aid have been inspired, on the one hand, by Samuel Smiles and his Victorian faith in individual effort and, on the other hand, by Peter Kropotkin, the anarchist and atheist who lived in Russia at the turn of the century.

In his work *Self Help with Illustrations of Character, Conduct and Perseverance*, Samuel Smiles famously declared:

> Heaven helps those who help themselves ... The spirit of self help is the root of all genuine growth in the individual; and exhibited in the lives of many, it constitutes the true source of national vigour and strength. Help from without is often enfeebling in its effects, but help from within invariably invigorates.

For Smiles, self help was essentially about individual and self-improvement, and antithetical to the activities of governments and charities. Kropotkin stressed the importance of collective action. In his book *Mutual Aid: A Factor of Evolution,*[1] he described mutual aid as a natural force which bound people together. Like Smiles, although for different reasons, Kropotkin rejected central and local state aid that imposed formal discipline and hierarchy. He also rejected the church and religion for preaching charity and thereby conferring superiority on the giver. But for him the essence of mutual aid was co-operative endeavour - an idea manifested in friendly societies, trade unions and the co-operative movement.

Since the 1970s, self help has been influenced by other forms of voluntary action, notably community development and the women's movement. Both have been committed to enabling individuals and groups to become more powerful and determine their own destinies, to gain in confidence and learn new skills, to stand up for their rights and to negotiate with professionals and others in authority. Their ideas and experience have helped to nourish the development of self help activities.

More recently, self help has become a symbol of renewal for civil society, a means of asserting autonomy and self determination for individuals and communities, against the centralising power of the state. The idea has been particularly salient in post-communist Eastern Europe, but also resonates in Western welfare states. The Czech President Vaclav Havel, writing in 1991, expressed this vision for the 21st century:

> The whole country will be criss-crossed by a network of local, regional and state-wide clubs, organisations, and associations with a wide variety of aims and purposes. This network will be so complex that it will be difficult to map thoroughly. Through it, the rich, nuanced and colourful life of a civilised European society will emerge and develop.[2]

Common characteristics

Self help groups are formed by people who, directly or through family or friends, have the same problem or life experience. They get together for mutual support and to share information and understanding. In a safe environment members of a group learn new ways of coping from each other. Individuals develop by being in the group through difficult times. People learn to give and take support, to value others and to feel valued themselves.

Essential characteristics of self help groups include informality, equality among members, a common concern and a decision to do something about this concern. Self help groups are often formed as a spontaneous response to an absence of services or to a hierarchical and formal organisation of services which people find unsatisfactory. Unlike statutory services or those provided by charitable organisations, self help groups are run by and for their members.

An elaborate definition is offered by the German Association of Self Help Supporters. Not all groups comply with the formula, but it covers the most common components of self help:

> Self help groups are voluntary, mostly loose associations of people whose activities are directed towards common coping with illnesses, psychological or social problems, by which they - either themselves personally or as relatives - are affected. They don't want to make a (commercial) profit. Their goal is a change in their personal life situation and often influence on their social and political environment. In regular, often weekly, groupwork they stress authenticity, equality, a common language and mutual aid. In doing so the group is a means to counteract outer (social) as well as inner (psychological) isolation. The goals of self help groups focus on their members, and not on outsiders; in that respect they differ from other forms of citizen's initiative. Self help groups are not led by professional helpers; some consult experts now and again on particular questions however.[3]

Core activities

Whether or not they fit this description precisely, all self help groups share certain core activities, which can be summarised as follows:

Emotional support

People join a self help group to give and receive support of a kind that can only be provided by others with similar experiences and problems.

Information

There is great need for clear, simple and appropriate information about the condition or problem around which the group is formed.

Most self help groups build up a small resource of literature and audio-visual material. Many produce their own leaflet or booklet to explain in accessible language the particular condition and suggest where to go for practical help. Another common strategy is to organise open meetings at which talks are given by professionals with specialist knowledge.

Advice and practical help

People who contact a self help group have queries and practical difficulties. Members of the group offer advice based on their own experience and their wider knowledge of the condition they share. Members often accompany each other on visits to hospitals and clinics, and increasingly self help groups run telephone helplines.

Recruiting

Most self help organisations, whether large or small, are concerned to recruit new members. Building membership is a way of adding to the group's store of knowledge about the conditions around which it is formed; it is also a way of spreading the knowledge it has to a wider range of people. Attracting members from different social and ethnic backgrounds can be a problem. Recruiting people from black and ethnic minority communities is a particular concern of many groups.

Publicity and education

Most groups publicise their meetings at some stage of their development in order to attract new members, to make themselves known to potential funders and to gain recognition among professionals. Leaflets, annual reports and newsletters are used to keep in touch with members and promote their activities. Groups use local radio, newsletters and journals to educate the wider public about their issue of concern. Giving talks to trainee and qualified professionals is a common activity.

Fundraising

Depending on how much money the group is hoping to raise, this activity varies from running jumble sales to applying for funds from charitable trusts.

Campaigning

Some groups undertake campaigning and lobby local councillors and MPs. There is a continuing debate among self help groups about how far they should get involved in campaigning and other pressure group activities. Some contend that trying to bring about change is a natural step to take when a group has identified bad practice or a lack of suitable services; in this sense, campaigning is seen as an extension of self help. Others maintain that self help is essentially about group members doing things for themselves and each other, and that campaigning for changes in the world beyond the group would contradict their purpose.

2. WHAT CAN SELF HELP ACHIEVE?

What can self help groups achieve for their members and for society at large? Here we use case studies to illustrate the main benefits which self help can bring to individuals and the ways in which groups can have a wider impact at local and national levels. We also consider their limitations.

Benefits for individual members

There are clearly a great many ways in which self help groups have an impact on their members. The following examples focus on two of the most common: ending isolation and lending practical support.

East London Cancer Group: Ending isolation

The first step in joining a group is to break the isolation that individuals feel when they experience a problem on their own. This is perhaps the most important benefit for anyone joining a self help group.

Vi Mitchell started a self help group in East London in 1979 when she came out of hospital after major surgery for cancer. She knew through her personal experience that there was no support locally other than individual families and friends. Anyone who came out of hospital after surgery was likely to feel isolated and to have little or no access to information or advice.

> There were five of us who had met at hospital having had surgery. Other people heard about the group. We did not advertise it anywhere. Word of mouth went around. There was so much need in the area. We were approached by new people all the time. We had to keep the numbers down. The maximum number my flat could take was 18. The others were turned away.

> The group gradually became a cancer group. We gave each other a lot of support. And we learned from others. People facing death or people learning to live with devastating effects of surgery. There was honesty and openness in the group. At times we all cried together. But we had evenings where each of us had to tell a funny story about something that happened in hospital.
>
> We had good fun discovering the various alternative cures practised in the USA. We dreamed of going to luxury hotels in Mexico and having new therapies. We argued about sugar versus honey. We discovered that Babycham sweetens the pills we had to take. The group had both men and women. We talked about sex. Some surgery destroys many people's ability to have sex. Nerves are sometimes severed in men and women often have their vagina affected. This wasn't the kind of conversation you could have anywhere else.

Credit Unions: Practical help for individuals

Some self help groups are concerned less with ending personal isolation than with providing practical support. Credit unions are a case in point. A credit union is a way of saving and borrowing money without using a bank. Members of the union save as much or as little as they want. This process keeps the money in the community. Loans are governed by each credit union's regulations. Most of the people who borrow money from a credit union could not go to a high street bank and ask for a loan. According to a study by the University of Sheffield[1] the number of credit unions trebled in three years to a total of over 200 in 1992. The researchers found that credit unions helped not only to alleviate debt problems but also, just as importantly, to bring communities together and to provide social and educational support.

One of the 22 founding members of the Rotten Park Winson Green credit union gives this account:

> I knew a little about credit unions in the West Indies. In some parts of Jamaica, where I come from, there are 14 or 15 miles before you can see a bank. Every district has a credit union office called Loan Bank, where farmers get loans before planting yellow banana or cane. The idea came from the Rotten Park Winson Green Employment Project. The suggestion struck a chord with everyone. Some people had heard about credit unions from Ireland where they are quite common. The Council was very keen and supportive.
>
> There was a lot to be done; recruiting members, learning how to run a credit union, registering as a Friendly Society. Within twelve months we had 100 members. The membership fee is £1. Then people can save whatever they can. Their ability to borrow depends on the consistency of their saving. Money is collected every week in a personal account. People are given a book which records their savings and shares. Annual dividends are calculated on the basis of profit margins. A member's request for a loan has to be approved by the Credit Committee, which decides according to the member's track record as well as their need.
>
> Members borrow to go on a holiday back home or to pay a high bill. For many of them the alternative would be a loan shark. Members get an annual dividend on savings even though they may still have an outstanding loan. Say you have shares of £200 and a loan of £150: you can pay the loan and increase savings or ask for a top-up loan to pay a high bill or deal with a crisis.
>
> When people get into bad debts we write to them. Ultimately the credit union could take them to the small claims court, but it does not happen very often. In the last

three or four years it only happened five times. The rate of bad debts is 0.35 per cent. Bank managers would be happy with a rate of 4-5 per cent. Unlike bank debts, credit union debts die with the borrower. All the policies are there to benefit the members.

Effecting wider changes

The activities of self help groups can do more than just benefit their own members. For example, if a group is successful in improving services there are gains for all users, whether or not they are members of the group. Some groups help to shift the balance of power from providers to users of public services; to influence public policy by bringing lay people's views to the attention of policy makers, to challenge established values and traditional roles, and to promote research. The following examples have been chosen to illustrate these functions, although it will be clear that there is considerable overlap between them.

Positively Women: Shifting power from providers to users

Positively Women was set up in 1987. Initially it was for women who, like its founder, had become HIV positive through drug use. The founder felt doubly isolated: women's AIDS groups excluded drug users and other groups consisted mainly of gay men. At first, women drug users responded to a poster advertising the group. Gradually they were joined by women infected through sexual activity, who eventually made up the majority of members. About 30 women participated in the first group with an average of 10-15 attending each fortnightly meeting. One of the members had experience in fund raising and together with the founder provided the drive, expertise and skills to set up an organisation which grew in six years from a small support group to a large London-wide organisation.

Positively Women runs a network of support groups, organises training days for women and service providers; distributes information, provides representatives for health and social services working parties; and raises awareness through the mass media about HIV and AIDS. It is funded by most London Boroughs and Health Authorities as well as by charitable foundations.

According to Positively Women, women find that from the moment of diagnosis, they are at the mercy of experts who are sometimes intolerant and judgmental. They feel powerless and out of control of their lives. They are sometimes pressed by social workers to tell their children about their illness, irrespective of their own ability to cope with the consequences. They are not always clear whether they are being given a new treatment for their own benefit or as part of a research exercise. Often their children are subjected to tests because, doctors argue, it can benefit research about the disease. African members of Positively Women are sometimes told by service providers that they are lucky to receive treatment and that they would not get it in their own country.

There is a general feeling among women that they are told what to do by professionals instead of being given information and choices. The way they are treated by service providers increases, rather than relieves, their sense of vulnerability. They therefore find it helpful to meet in a setting where there is support, trust and respect for confidentiality.

The support groups run by Positively Women are exclusively for HIV positive women. Feeling safe to be open about HIV is very important for the women who come to the groups. Each group has a paid worker who is also HIV positive, trained to facilitate the group, organise the activities and provide counselling. The groups meet between from 11 am and 3 pm so that women can take their children to and from school.

In addition to sharing experiences and giving and receiving support, women can have training in safer sex, assertiveness, counselling skills and coping with loss and bereavement. Newly diagnosed women have the opportunity to meet others who are living with HIV. The groups build up information about symptoms, ways of coping, different therapies and their side effects.

Positively Women has built up a wealth of knowledge which they use to influence professionals in health and social care. Members give talks to professionals, organise presentations at conferences and seminars, act as consultants to professional bodies, work with the media to promote awareness and produce health education for specific groups of vulnerable women such as women in prisons and hostels. The organisation is represented on the Medical Research Council's Collaborative Study of HIV in Women.

The Grandparents' Federation: Influencing public policy

The Grandparents' Federation was founded in 1987, two years after a group of grandparents got together to share their concern about the plight of grandparents who had no contact with their grandchildren. Most of their difficulties occurred when children were taken into care and grandparents were forbidden to help in a family crisis.

The Federation was set up with funds from Children in Need and Age Concern, in order to respond to telephone calls and letters from grandparents seeking advice and support. Further grants have since been secured to finance specific projects. Membership is open to anyone, regardless of creed or colour, who shares its aims and objectives. Members receive a quarterly newsletter and information about meetings. People join because they feel powerless to influence social services, resentful about their lack of legal rights and unjustly deprived of their grandchildren through no fault of their own. They also experience the stigma attached to families with children in care, who are so often assumed to have been abused by their parents.

The Grandparents' Federation campaigned to raise public awareness about the range of reasons why families break up, including mental illness and long hospital stays. They highlighted, through personal stories, the contribution grandparents make when they are allowed to help look after their grandchildren. They involved retired social workers in their support groups, who acted as advocates for families and provided a bridge between them and the professionals.

Members of the Grandparents' Federation lobbied MPs who were debating the Bill which became the 1989 Children Act. The Act simplifies and rationalises the grandparents' position in seeking contact, particularly with children in care. It is also helpful to grandparents in internal family disputes. It became clear that grandparents would need help in order to benefit from the legislation. The Federation continues to offer support, advice and information. It is involved in a pilot project in Newcastle to enable people to act as surrogate grandparents for children in care. Having started life as a single self help group, it is now a national organisation striving to develop a network of local self help groups.

Southall Black Sisters and the Everyman Centre: Challenging established values

Domestic violence has been described as part of a wider social, institutional and political framework that "subordinates women, trivialises their abuse and addicts men to the maintenance of power and control over them". Southall Black Sisters in West London and the Everyman Centre in Brixton, South London, are two organisations which help individuals involved in domestic violence to change their behaviour. In doing so they challenge the values that prevail in the communities to which the individuals belong, as well as in society at large.

Southall Black Sisters was set up in 1979 to address the needs of Black, Asian, African and Caribbean women. They carry out casework, advocacy and counselling with women facing violence and abuse at home. The majority of their clients are Asian women. They have found that women and girls who experience violence in their families have been traumatised and often suffer from depression and suicidal tendencies as a result. Many are also under pressure to conform to cultural and religious norms and values.

The support they give to Asian women and girls is met with disapproval by many Asian men and local institutions. For challenging the status of women within the family and the community at large, Southall Black Sisters are criticised for letting the community down and for losing their ethnic and cultural identity. In response, they cite evidence that domestic violence damages women's mental health and argue that the services available to them are not providing appropriate support. They are seeking to develop innovative models of intervention.

The Everyman Centre is a project run by men offering a range of support services for men who want to stop behaving violently. It is based in Brixton in South London and accepts men from London and the neighbouring counties. More than 250 men were seen at the Centre in the first two years (1991-93).

The Everyman Centre recognises that many factors may contribute to a man's violent behaviour but that he always has a choice. Violence is neither inevitable nor inherent. The Centre's counselling programme consists of a combination of short term individual counselling followed by a further three months of group work. The aim is to challenge and change the attitudes and behavioural patterns of men, to redress male stereotyping and to foster understanding of power dynamics and inequalities. Men must choose to attend the Centre; they are not referred by outside agencies. Men from different backgrounds are encouraged to help each other in a safe, careful environment.

The British Diabetic Association: Promoting research

The British Diabetic Association (BDA), set up in 1934, is a lay association which provides a number of services including support for self help groups. It represents the interests of people with diabetes and maintains contact with them through local branches and groups. It has three main objectives:

- To provide education and information for people with diabetes and their professional advisers.

- To represent the interests and welfare of people with diabetes.

- To promote research into the causes, prevention and cure of diabetes.

The Association provides an umbrella for self help groups formed around diabetes. It helps them get in touch with each other and provides training for members and group leaders. It has more than 400 local groups in the UK. These groups provide a local point of contact for people with diabetes and their families. They also raise funds for BDA and to provide equipment for a local diabetic clinic or day unit.

BDA recognises that the diagnosis of diabetes comes as a major shock to the individuals concerned, causing loss of self esteem and undermining their view of themselves as competent and healthy. By sharing and venting feelings in a group with other diabetics, they can regain confidence, become competent in dealing with diabetes and form a new image of themselves which feels comfortable.

According to a study undertaken for BDA in 1990[2], group members found it helpful to share personal difficulties including feelings of anger and anxiety about the disease. There was a mutual understanding about not always doing the right thing: a degree of non-compliance to the demands of diabetes was seen as necessary for a full life.

There have been some attempts to set up groups outside BDA for those who felt it was not catering for their needs. For example, some women with diabetes felt that BDA only mentioned women in relation to pregnancy. There was also a view among young people that their needs were overshadowed by those of older people and parents of diabetic children. Members of ethnic minorities found that diets suggested by BDA took no account of their culinary traditions. In response the organisation has been trying to broaden its scope and devote space in the newsletter to issues such as these. However, at the time of writing, financial difficulties had caused BDA to cut back some of its services and give priority to research.

Limitations

For all the benefits they offer, self help groups are not suitable for everybody. For many people it is bad enough thinking about their own problems let alone listening to other people's. Some think that participating in a self help group would simply increase their preoccupation with their own difficulties. Others worry that self help groups, particularly for people with learning difficulties, may make them more stigmatised by isolating them further from the rest of society.

Like other forms of social gathering self help groups harbour as much opportunity for conflict as for positive development. As members draw closer to each other and become more committed to the group, the chance for disagreement and conflict increases. Some groups have 'difficult members' who can be disruptive. When individuals become disappointed with a self help group, this can exacerbate the problems which brought them to the group in the first place. A common difficulty is finding members who are willing to take on organising tasks. The same few people do all the work while others seem to get only the benefits. For example, a group's treasurer often occupies this position year after year because nobody else wants it.

Signs of fragility and informality in self help groups may worry professionals who wish to protect their patients or clients from negative experiences. Doctors may worry about misinformation and confusion or even crankiness in a group, or about groups being too dogmatic about how members should help themselves. These fears reflect the gulf between expert and experiential knowledge and are rarely founded in fact. Professionals do not always take kindly to lay people criticising or supplementing the services they provide. They may feel threatened by self help groups if they see them as pressure groups prepared to campaign for change. We explore the relationship between self help groups and professionals in more detail later on (p.51).

There are, of course, some practical limits to the effectiveness of self help groups. When members are unwell, tired or live far away from each other their contribution to the group is severely cut back. People with few resources and little access to information may not be able to bring into the group what it needs in order to develop. These limitations are more marked in self help groups in rural areas and among disadvantaged communities. We discuss support for self help in these and other conditions on p.47.

3. SCOPE AND DEVELOPMENT OF SELF HELP ACTIVITIES

In this section we offer a fuller picture of the scope of self help. First we show how it links a range of other activities which are similar though distinct from self help. Next we consider how self help activities are adapted to suit different categories of need. We then chart the development of self help from a simple group structure to larger and more complex organisations with wider objectives.

Associated activities

Self help can be seen as part of a wider spectrum of lay activity in health and social issues, ranging from individual self care to collective campaigning. It links and overlaps with all of the following functions:

Self care

Increasingly people want to know more about how to look after themselves. Alternatives to conventional medicine such as aromatherapy and special diets have caught people's imagination. This new interest is reflected in a growing volume of literature. Self care is an individual activity, but is often encouraged among members of self help groups as one of the ways they learn to cope with their condition.

Group therapy

Professionally led therapy groups for people who share the same health or social concern (such as an eating disorder) often function rather like a self help group. People express their feelings and anxieties to each other and provide mutual support. In a therapy group, unlike a self help group, the therapist remains in charge.

Befriending

This involves matching somebody with a mental or physical health problem, or with learning difficulties, with a volunteer to provide support and help over a period of time. The 'buddy' system for AIDS sufferers is one example. Unlike a self help group, befriending is about one-to-one relationships. Some self help groups operate befriending schemes and they can be a way of introducing new members to a group.

Advocacy

Disadvantaged people are paired with ordinary citizens who are able to support them in claiming their rights and negotiating with service providers. Advocacy schemes have been set up around people with mental health problems and learning difficulties, and for ethnic minority women using maternity services. Advocacy can be an important adjunct and means to self help.

Community development

This can be understood as the process by which a community defines its own needs and negotiates with service providers about how to meet them. Community projects involved in health and social issues mushroomed in the 1980s, but more recently they have suffered from a lack of funding. Community health projects are a form of community development and many of these support self help groups. For example, the Wells Park Health Project in the London Borough of Lewisham supports a swimming group for elderly women, an HIV group, an irritable bowel syndrome group, a slimming group, a carers' group and two reminiscence groups. Community development is more outward-looking than self help and more concerned with bringing about practical change in local services.

Lay participation in local decision-making

Individuals and representatives of interest groups become members of panels and committees discussing policy and service provision in many parts of health and social services. Currently, user involvement is actively encouraged by the Government and self help groups are increasingly asked to provide representatives for national or local bodies.

Campaigning

As we have noted, campaigning is a common function among self help groups. It is of course undertaken by many organisations which are not involved in self help. It is seen by some as an extension of self help and by others as undermining the principle of self reliance which is thought to be central to self help.

Adapting self help to different categories of need

Self help groups can be described in six major categories: physical illness, disability, mental health, carers' groups, addiction and social issues. There are overlaps - for example, where a disability is due to a physical illness - and some groups fit into more than one category. However, it is useful to consider the categories separately, both to appreciate the enormous range of self help activity, and to understand that, while all groups have aims and activities in common, they nevertheless have distinctive characteristics and priorities which are tailored to the particular experiences of their members.

The concerns and activities of groups formed around physical illness will vary according to the nature of the disease. Disability groups tend to look outwards: their preoccupation is with changing attitudes in a society which is ignorant or careless of the needs of disabled people. Mental health groups form around powerlessness: their members have lost control over their lives and want to regain it. Carers' groups aim to give carers an identity and gain recognition for the work they do. Groups formed around addictions tend to be preoccupied with problems associated with stigmatisation and illegality. The final category includes a broad range of groups, some with specific and others with more general concerns: these change as social attitudes and conditions change; new groups form as new issues become visible.

What follows is not an exhaustive account of self help activity. For example, there are self help groups around employment, housing and homelessness, whose important activities could not be included in this study. Housing co-operatives, tenants' associations and self build are some of the self help initiatives in the housing field; the Homeless Network[1] is an alliance of agencies including self help initiatives.

Physical illness

Self help groups form around both chronic and life threatening conditions. The national database set up by Help for Health[2] lists 1,500 groups and associations dealing with common ailments and rare diseases.

Individuals diagnosed with an illness join a self help group to break their isolation, to share their worries and to find out more about their condition. A newly diagnosed person may be beset by fears and feel there are too many questions to ask the doctor. They need information, support, sympathy and practical help, as the following accounts of two women diagnosed with cancer suggest:

> I was 37 years old and I had breast cancer. I was in a state of shock. I gave myself up to the doctors and the hospital. I blocked my anger. I sat for hours waiting. All I could think of was that I wanted it done and over with. I did not think of asking any questions or getting information from anybody. I went to the operation theatre not knowing what was going to happen. The doctor said it would depend on what they find. I asked the nurse how would I know if I had a mastectomy. She said that after a mastectomy I would have a blood transfusion. No need for words. I saw the drip and I knew.

> I went to hospital to have a colostomy without being given any information about it. Nobody told me what it was, where it would go, or how my life style would change. At hospital they gave me no advice on how to take care of myself. They needed my bed and sent me home too soon. One of the difficulties with cancer is that it is a changing illness. You have to prepare yourself for the next problem. When I came back home I was very ill, I had no control over my bowel, I could not walk more than a few steps at the time, I was wondering how long I was going to be alive. I learned more from other people with cancer and from the Colostomy Association than from the medical staff who looked after me. I found out I could get appliances and practical help.

Both women joined local cancer support groups they identified through national organisations. Others have had to start their own groups because there was nothing appropriate in their locality. Starting a new group requires time, commitment and some money. It may take time to recruit members. A newly diagnosed condition, on the other hand, can attract media attention and bring in a rush of new members. When a member of ME Action (Myalgic Encephalomyelitis is a stress-related illness. Little is known about what causes it and how to cure it) wrote an article about the illness in the *Observer*, it started an avalanche of publicity and membership shot up from 500 to 10,000 in the space of two years.

A national survey carried out by CancerLink in 1992 charted the activities of 350 cancer support and self help groups. We reproduce their findings below, since they are considered typical of most self help groups in the area of physical illness. They are listed in the order of activities carried out by most groups.

Table 1

CANCER SUPPORT GROUP ACTIVITIES BY PERCENTAGE

Activity	%
LIBRARY	92
BEFRIENDING	89
INFORMATION	88
TELEPHONE SUPPORT	88
ONE TO ONE SUPPORT	79
HOME VISITING	79
HOSPITAL VISITING	79
OPEN GROUP MEETINGS	70
SOCIAL ACTIVITIES	64
TALKS TO GROUPS	55
COMPLEMENTARY THERAPIES	45
NEWSLETTER	38
TRANSPORT TO HOSPITAL	37
CLOSED GROUP MEETINGS	35
REPRESENTATION	21
CAMPAIGNING	18
PUBLICITY IN ETHNIC PRESS	11

Source: Celebrating Groups: The results of a national survey of cancer support and self help groups, Cancerlink 1992.

The survey found that as groups matured, they became more outward looking and increasingly attempt to influence service provision locally for people affected by cancer.

Disability

Some of the self help groups formed around physical illnesses include disabled people in their membership. Their disabilities are a direct result of their illness or surgery. The action and the debate around self help and disability, however, is not so much about what to do with the impairment itself as how to fight against prejudice and discrimination.

In the 1990s there is a growing movement of disabled people who insist that their lives have value and who want to be treated as equal citizens with equal rights. They are challenging stereotypes, fighting for access to jobs and services, and finding a voice in politics and culture. The movement of disabled people also challenges charities run by non-disabled people on the ground that they perpetuate segregation and dependency. They want organisations run by disabled people for disabled people according to the principles of self help and mutual aid.

Independent Living is a term used to describe their objectives: "the way we want to live our lives, our wish to play an equal and full role in the communities we live in." Margaret Edwards was in institutional care for 28 years and moved to her own home at the age of 44:

> My first night here my friend stopped with me. I wouldn't say I was frightened but it was strange. But the second night she had gone. And I had this wonderful feeling. I thought I can get up when I want, I can go to bed when I want, I can have a drink or something to eat when I want.[3]

Conventional ideas about independence are considered inappropriate, as Jenny Morris, a disabled and feminist researcher and writer on disability issues, explains:

> In Western industrial societies, this term has commonly been associated with the ability to do things for oneself, to be self-supporting, self-reliant. When physical impairment means that there are things that someone cannot do for themselves, daily living tasks with which they need help, the assumption is that this person is 'dependent'... to be dependent is to be subordinate, to be subject to the control of others.

In her book, *Independent Lives*, she quotes a definition of independence:

> In a practical and commonsense way to mean simply being able to achieve our goals. The point is that independent people have control over their lives, not that they perform every task themselves. Independence is not linked to the physical or intellectual capacity to care for oneself without assistance, independence is created by having assistance when and how one requires it.[4]

In various ways in the 1980s and 1990s, disabled people took control over their own care. Centres for Independent Living (CIL) in Britain were inspired by an initiative in California, where disabled people set up their own centre, which they controlled. The centres are run by disabled people with the help of non-disabled employees. For example, Hampshire CIL helps people who need personal assistance control how that assistance is provided. This means helping people to recruit and manage employees, negotiate funding and deal with tax and national insurance. All these are skills which disabled people acquire and pass on to others.

Common threads can be found between organisations of physically disabled people and those of people with learning difficulties such as People First. This was set up in 1984 inspired by similar groups in the USA. According to one of its founders, Gary Boule, it is "more than a self help group":

> It is a pressure group set up to challenge services and charities, to campaign in order to get rid of labelling and, eventually, to run services. It remains fundamentally a self help group because it helps its members develop self confidence and get their problems off their chest.

People First use self advocacy, where individuals speak on their own behalf or are supported by another disabled person, to develop their confidence and achieve their aims. Members of People First include those living in the community and in institutions. They want access to housing and jobs. They have good links with similar groups in Australia and other parts of the world where the disabled people's movement has made considerable progress.

The British Council of Organisations of Disabled People (BCODP) was formed in 1981 to harness the growing consciousness of disabled people, to redefine the problem of disability, and to give a focus to campaigns for independent living and against discrimination. It was conceived and developed without extensive financial support from government or from traditional organisations for disabled people. It now represents more than 75 organisations of disabled people and some 200,000 disabled individuals.

Care in the community theoretically offers an opportunity for disabled people to leave institutions and become more independent. In reality, community care often means dependence on inadequate services or on relatives, and imprisonment within the four walls of one's home. Local organisations of disabled people provide practical help and support; campaigning activities; training courses in specific skills and self confidence.

Mental health and well being

This category covers a wide range of activities, from prevention of mental illness to dealing with phobias and life crises such as bereavement. Many women's groups function as preventative mental health groups. Some groups give themselves names such as Spectrum or the Wednesday Group to avoid stigma. Others find that they want to 'own' their illness as part of the process of coping and name their group accordingly, for instance by calling it a manic depressives group.

People join mental health groups because they need help and in order to help others. They may have tried the doctor or psychiatrist, but they still need understanding and support. For some people the motivation to join or set up a mental health group is anger. Many people who have been subjected to psychiatric treatment experienced powerlessness. Joining a group is a way of regaining control over one's life. Reaching out to those with a shared experience breaks away from being a victim encouraged to refer to experts for help.

Groups formed by survivors, as people who have endured psychiatric treatment call themselves, usually develop advocacy schemes, organise campaigns to raise awareness around human rights of psychiatric patients and seek to change the way services are delivered for the benefit of others. The national umbrella organisation MIND includes such groups and initiatives among its members.

Other groups focus more on mutual aid and self development than on advocacy and campaigning. They constitute the mainstream of self help groups in mental health. One example is the Eating Disorders Association (EDA). Eating disorders have one of the highest mortality rates of all psychiatric illness: more than ten per cent of sufferers die, according to EDA, from the effects of starvation or from suicide. Anorexia and bulimia are secretive illnesses which usually originate in adolescence and mainly affect young women. The few specialist treatment centres in the UK can help a total of 1,500 people every year, while the estimated number of sufferers is more than 150,000. Eating disorders are widely misunderstood, even by doctors and little help for sufferers is available at a local level, except through self help groups.

Anorexic Aid and Anorexic Family Aid merged to form the EDA in 1989. Its headquarters, funded by the Department of Health and several charitable trusts and businesses, are in Norwich. Since 1992 EDA has also incorporated the Society for the Advancement of Research into Anorexia (SARA). EDA aims to help everyone who is involved with anorexia or bulimia, including sufferers, their families and friends, and professionals caring for them. The organisation offers telephone helplines, a network of local self help groups and contacts, a professional journal published twice yearly, and information booklets and leaflets about the disorder.

The need for understanding is the main motive for joining a group, as this young woman's account illustrates:

> When I became anorexic in my early teens, exercising obsessively came hand in hand with starving myself. What little I did eat, I earned through exercising. During my teenage years and my early 20s, I would run for over 100 miles a week and pedal for up to four hours a day on the hardest gear of my exercise bike. My mind was blinkered, my feelings numbed - I knew or understood nothing outside this all consuming need in me to live my life in this way.
>
> When people say to me 'Aren't you good keeping fit all the time?' I find their comments very hard to swallow. Their words always seem so full of admiration, even envy, yet they are spoken in ignorance of the devastating and destructive part that exercise has played in my life.

EDA has over more than 40 self help groups. Most are open to family and friends as well as sufferers, and are led by volunteers who are recovered sufferers, carers or professionals. These leaders are known as Contacts. In addition to the network of self help groups, EDA keeps a register of Contacts who agree to make themselves available to sufferers and carers through letters, telephone, or meetings on a one-to-one basis.

Eating disorders groups offer friendship, understanding and hope: "people can say how they really feel in a secure environment." Beyond this fundamental service to their members, groups vary in the activities they organise. Some are part of a more comprehensive project offering counselling, a library and a telephone helpline. Others simply meet to discuss ways of coping with an eating disorder and how to ask for help. Many groups organise talks on topics such as sexual abuse, body image and anger. Groups are also concerned with raising public awareness around eating disorders. Giving talks to professionals is part of most groups' activities.

In Derbyshire Dales District there is a federation of mental health groups. Their activities reflect the wide range of needs among local people. Some organise social outings such as TAG, Thursday Activity Group, while others run art classes, or meet regularly to respond to the need for support, or focus on specific problems such as 'drinking to cope' and Alzheimer's disease.

The following testimonies are from members of self help groups in Derbyshire Dales:

> I first got involved in a self-help group five years ago, when my husband died and a neighbour suggested I join a group. I was at a low ebb but not seriously ill. I liked going out of the village where everybody knew me and I did not feel I could talk about my personal problems. Our group meets in Bakewell. To begin with it was a nice night out. I felt useful to the other members because I could give some of them a lift in my car. Later I joined another group that meets in the day to help each other with shopping or going somewhere. Sometimes we make things to sell and raise a little money for the group.

> When I first came out of hospital I liked the informality of the group. I needed to talk. Now I also enjoy the more formal groups where we learn something. I am a member of the women's group. There are about ten women at the meetings. We do art therapy, massage and relaxation. I also attend a day group where we play board games. The creative writing group is another one. It has six members and we all write something to read out to everyone.

> I joined a group a long time ago in 1984. It was suggested to me by the Community Mental Health Team. To begin with I was apprehensive, but there were six of us and we stayed together. We had support from an outreach worker, but we did not want him to run the group... You get motivated in a group. We talked about ECT once. There was a lot of anger expressed about having things done to you. Other meetings were more fun. Somebody would come with a guitar and sing... In another meeting one of the members told us her story. It was a dreadful experience of incest which she told in a state of emotional tension to an audience of 25 people. It is surprising to see the degree of intimacy that can develop in a group. This requires enormous trust and confidence.

Addiction

This category includes what is perhaps the single best known self help group, Alcoholics Anonymous (AA). AA have branches in 115 countries and approximately 70,000 groups, all following the same rules. Other addictions around which there are self help groups include illegal drug abuse and legally prescribed drugs such as tranquillisers. The illegality of the former combined with a lack of resources available for drug related projects, make it difficult for people with drug problems to set up self help groups. 'Tranx' groups, meanwhile, are growing in numbers.

AA was formed in the United States in 1935 by a New York stockbroker and an Ohio surgeon, both alcoholics. They found that meeting and talking together helped them stay sober. The desire to give up drinking is still the reason for joining an AA group. Members are helped to achieve sobriety by staying away from one drink, one day at a time.

Newcomers to an AA group are encouraged to follow 12 steps, based on the common belief "once an alcoholic, always an alcoholic". The emphasis is on the individual, who must accept that they are powerless over alcohol, but that their sanity can be restored with the help of a power greater than themselves. The 12 steps seek to establish a belief in God and a commitment to self improvement. Like other self help groups AA groups provide mutual support and the opportunity to share experiences and learn new ways of coping. Unlike other self help groups, AA groups don't act as pressure groups or campaign for changes in government policy towards alcohol.

The services offered by AA consist of a general service office and telephone lines throughout the country. Members are also offered an international network of support. Each group is self financing. Members contribute what they can to cover expenses such as literature, coffee and tea, and rental of meeting rooms. The groups also contribute to the general service office which is run by paid staff.

An AA group of doctors in the United States who were interviewed about their recovery from alcoholism emphasised another important aspect of their experience: "the experience of recovery humanises us... We are no longer self-centred and better than everybody. We are human."

Others highlighted the importance of the spiritual dimension of AA meetings. This is of particular relevance to people with medical and therefore scientific training. In the words of one member of this group:

> Our scientific training makes us want to know the reason for everything. Once you don't have to know the reason for everything, you're coming home, baby, you're really coming home.[5]

A survey was carried out in Britain in 1988[6] to assess the rate of recovery among members of a self help group (not AA) for doctors and dentists who had problems with alcohol and drug misuse. Out of 100 doctors who joined the group at some point between 1980 and 1988, 76 were found to have abstained from alcohol for over six months. The remaining 24 people in the sample include three who admitted not to have recovered, 12 who died in the meantime and the rest lost touch.

In 1990 the Scottish Drugs Forum identified a need for support groups for relatives of illegal drug users and for a community-based approach to the rehabilitation of drug users. The members of the Forum found it surprising how little the traditional self help movement has concerned itself with drug issues. They attributed this to poverty, discrimination and illegality.

It has been suggested that there should be centres in neighbourhoods with high misuse of drugs such as opiates and 'crack' cocaine to function as drop-in facilities, to provide information to relatives, to produce health education for the community, counselling, medical advice, and other general advice on housing and jobs. Such a resource could also support self help groups and organise volunteers to help. However, funds are not available for this type of service. It has been easier to set up groups for parents, siblings and friends of drug abusers. Research in the late 1980s[7] found that self help groups for drug users' families are concentrated in London, the North West and Scotland. Families Anonymous, an organisation that supports groups along the lines of Alcoholics Anonymous, helped in setting up most of the groups in the research sample. The researcher identified clear benefits for those participating in the groups and possible benefits for the drug users themselves:

> The majority of groups in our study had come into existence because of one or more founder members had felt aggrieved at the way they were dealt with by the agencies with which their child or partner had been in contact. Since there was no service specifically for families and feelings of guilt and stigma made them very reticent about voicing discontent to friends or making their views public, they took matters into their own hands and set up groups themselves. We have already seen that leaders mentioned reduced isolation, mutual support and the sense of sharing and empathy as being an important part of what groups had to offer and these can be seen as giving immediate relief.

The study also highlighted the particular problems attached to HIV contracted through the use of contaminated syringes. Drug users' support groups are having to find their own ways of responding to their members' needs. As Bill Nelles, a consultant to Berkshire Health Authority explains:

> Gay men have sometimes related to drug users either as a stereotyped group of criminals and psychological misfits, to be politely shunted off to special facilities or, more fraternally, as another persecuted minority. Both points of view can be equally misguided.[8]

Mainliners, the largest of the AIDS/drugs self help groups was founded in 1988 with funds from the National AIDS Trust. In trying to set up self help groups, founding members of Mainliners realised that before drug addicts could help each other and themselves they needed an organisation offering practical help as well as emotional support.

A cry for help received recently by the Nottingham Self Help Team came from a tranquilliser 'tranx' group: "People need more help than we can give." Nottingham Self Help Team sponsored research[9] into services for people dependent on tranquillisers in Nottinghamshire. It was found that tranx groups offered a variety of activities such as relaxation, exercise, outings, home visits, telephone helplines, advocacy and information, and that the groups provided essential support for their members. The Tranquillisers Forum was set up to prevent new cases of dependence, to support people who are users, and to promote co-operation between agencies, professionals and users. Local self help groups formed around tranquillisers are working together in Nottingham. One of their first initiatives has been the production of a leaflet entitled *Tranquillisers - the facts*. Funding has been provided by Nottinghamshire Social Services and Nottingham Health Authority Simple Small Grants. Already, a worker is in post and the Family Health Services Authority have changed their guidelines for prescribing practices.

Carers' groups

Carers are people who look after somebody who is frail, disabled or severely ill. This person could be a child with a disability or an elderly or disabled relative or close friend. Carers can be on duty 24 hours a day, seven days a week, yet the contribution they make is not fully recognised either by the carers themselves or by society as a whole. This is partly due to the fact that caring is part of a relationship which creates and justifies the carer's obligations. In this respect being a carer is different from being a nurse or home help.

There are six million carers in Britain, 1.7 million of whom live with the person they look after. And yet, according to Carers' National Association, only 110,000 receive invalid care allowance. There are many problems with this particular allowance, but the low number of people who receive it must be partly due to the non-recognition of caring as a legitimate service.

Looking after somebody who is disabled or elderly may cause tensions in the relationship between the carer and the person being looked after. Moral obligation and guilt are part of this relationship. Pressures such as not being able to maintain a job or becoming isolated add to the burden of the carer. The carer's health often takes second place to the needs of the person being cared for. Carers need support and, increasingly, they are finding it in the company of other carers.

The following account in *Community Care*[10] magazine is shared by many carers:

> Anne Murrain looks after her 81 year old father at home. He has been a diabetic for 28 years and is partially sighted. She gives him his insulin injections and helps him around the house. "When I first started looking after him I felt I was alone. I was never told of any service that could help me. It's hard, strenuous work.
>
> In 1990 Anne joined the Black Carers Support Group set up in the Annie Wood Resource Centre in Birmingham. The initiative to form a group specifically for Afro-Caribbean carers came from a social worker, a district nurse and a community worker. They felt that, as among white carers, there was a lack of information among black people about services and welfare benefits available to carers. A group could help with informing and supporting them.
>
> The group meets every three weeks and organises a social outing once a year. More than anything else, the group gives an opportunity for its members to discuss their problems and to share them - realising that someone else has to deal with similar issues can be uplifting... they feel more comfortable among other black people where they can speak their patois. It also allows the members to socialise, share recipes, and discuss issues relating to the black community or home background which they might feel constrained to mention in a predominantly white group.

Carers' groups can either be general for any carer irrespective of who they are looking after or specifically for people who care for relatives with the same illness or disability, such as the Alzheimer's Disease Society (ADS).

ADS was set up in 1979 to support the families of those who have Alzheimer's disease; to provide advice and information on the disease; to give guidance and training to both carers and professionals; to promote research; and to press for improved services. Their income comes mostly from subscriptions. The organisation also receives grants including one from the Department of Health.

ADS has 13 regional offices who maintain a network of branches and groups. Sally Knocker, the regional officer for the London region, describes the support she offers to groups:

> In London there are 12 ADS branches. Each branch supports a number of carers' groups and may be involved in fundraising, campaigning, running day centres and providing respite care. In addition to the branches, there are seven free-standing groups in my region. We keep a directory of all the groups with a contact name and telephone number which we give out to carers wanting to join a group locally. We provide guidelines and starter packs for the groups' main organisers. We also organise meetings for them to share some of their concerns about the groups. For example, the issues discussed at the latest meeting included: how to involve new carers; how to avoid cliquishness in a group; and how to meet the needs of carers of people in different stages of the disease.
>
> Some groups are set up for a fixed period of eight to ten weeks during which they have a programme of talks including information giving on items such as benefits, help, services and coping with stress. At the same time, groups are giving and receiving support. At the end of this fixed period of time the group decides whether or not to continue. Some groups go on for a long time. I can think of an example of a group that has been meeting the first Wednesday every month for eight years. It is organised by an 86-year-old woman who receives from ten to 19 members in her living room.

> The essence of self help is to let people learn new skills while they are doing everything themselves, but many carers ask for somebody else to take responsibility to organise the group. We provide them with a facilitator, who is usually an ex-carer or a professional, or, less often, a carer. In the future, we may develop very specific groups for daughters and sons who have different needs from spouses. They are younger, most of them do not live with their parent, and they are used to being cared for by their parent and find it difficult to change roles.

Social issues

Among those who form self help groups in this category are lone parents, victims of domestic violence or sexual abuse and families of offenders. People in these circumstances often feel isolated and need to share experiences. They get together in self help groups to give and take support.

For example, the Child Abuse Studies Unit (CASU) was set up at the University of North London in 1987 to research child sexual abuse. They found that they had to widen their brief to include domestic violence and all forms of sexual violence. They carry out research, offer teaching, training and public speaking, and give counselling and information to individuals.

Through their work, CASU are in touch with many local services such as therapy centres and rape crisis centres. Most of them offer support to self help groups, which have been found to make a valuable contribution by helping people who have been sexually abused to recover from the experience.

CASU have identified three types of groups: groups that are organised and facilitated by outsiders such as counsellors; groups that are organised but not facilitated by an outsider; and 'ad hoc' groups that are set up by an individual who wants to start a group.

Groups in the first two categories are set up by a variety of service providers including women's centres, social services departments, rape crisis centres and psychiatric departments. Those facilitated by a trained therapist are closed and have a fixed timescale, such as 12 weeks or six months. Where group members do not wish to have a professional facilitator, they decide whether or not to be a closed group and set their own time limits; usually, at least one member already has experience of running a group. 'Ad hoc' groups are set up by individuals who wish to share feelings and experiences with others. This kind of group is likely to be advertised on a notice board of a GP practice or a women's centre. Sometimes people hear about a group on the grapevine. The monthly newsletter *Incest & Child Sexual Assault* has information about new groups.

Many people who have experienced sexual abuse ask for one-to-one counselling or therapy. Rasjida St John, who has worked with groups of sexually abused women for 12 years, argues that a self help group can do much more for the individual than a therapist.

> Sexual abuse is something survivors have to deal with for themselves. The help they may receive from a therapist is very limited. Often they have an illusion of being helped. Whereas in a self help group they talk to others with similar experiences and find the support they need in order to take responsibility for dealing with the abuse. A self help group is better for the person's self esteem. This is different from the attitude expressed by some people who say: "I have been damaged. Someone has to come to my rescue." Furthermore, every individual experiences their abuse in a particular way. There is no point in medicalising sexual abuse by turning it into a new type of illness and looking for therapies to cure it.

The advantages of a self help group over one-to-one therapy include: members of the group know they are not alone; they realise that sexual abuse is a social problem - one in five women and one in 14 men have been abused in some way during their childhood according to CASU; the topic is discussed within a broad social context; in a group people develop strategies to cope with what has happened to them; groups offer a social network as well as help with the particular issue; and self help groups don't cost participants any money.

A practical difficulty for professionals who want to recommend that their patients or clients join a self help group is that information about groups changes rapidly and is often out of date. It is difficult to know exactly which groups are closed, which run from which date to which date and might still be open, and where there might be publicity for a new group. The facilitators may not be there when they are needed. This difficulty is overcome where there are good information networks and service providers work closely with voluntary sector projects.

Development of self help groups

The following case studies show how self help groups develop in different ways, from simple beginnings to larger and more complex organisations. First we look at the stages of development that are common to most self help groups and at the life cycle of a local self help group; next we consider how larger organisations have grown up to provide a range of functions, from national campaigning, to supporting local groups and liaising with professionals to provide services.

Stages of development

Whatever their aims, all groups go through similar stages. Tuckman[11] describes four stages for groups to work through in order to become productive. They are:

Forming	getting together
Storming	identifying differences
Norming	agreeing direction and activities
Performing	working productively

Some groups may go through these stages many times as the membership changes and some groups get stuck in the early stages of 'forming' and 'storming'. An understanding of these stages can help members make sense of what is happening in their group. In addition, members need to develop skills which ensure that the group is meeting the needs of the individuals, achieving its purpose and attending to the process of working constructively together. A facilitator can help with this, as well as with understanding the stages of development.

Life cycle of a local group

Contact-a-Family (CaF) was set up in 1979 to encourage mutual support among families whose children have special needs, regardless of the type of disability experienced by the children. It is funded by the Department of Health, a number of local authorities and charitable trusts and corporate bodies. This account shows how self help activities evolve, from the moment when an individual decides to seek out a group.

CaF maintains that joining a self help group is a decision of great significance:

> It involves acknowledgement by the joiner that he or she has the problem with which the group is concerned, and this raises what may be deep-seated questions about the joiner's identity. Thus in the case of CaF it requires recognition that the joiner's child is part of the handicapped world. These may be large steps to take psychologically.

In practical terms the decision to set up a new group or look for one that is already there usually stems from the deeply felt personal experiences of one or two parents. Parents often talk of isolation, loneliness, and feelings of being the only one with a special needs child. Anger and disappointment at feeling without relevant support at a time of great need can motivate people to seek out others in similar situations.

It is not always easy to identify other parents who would like to join a group. The methods vary from chance meetings within a clinic or hospital waiting room to notices in newsagents' windows and local press. Asking professionals to give out information about the group receives a variety of responses ranging from positive encouragement to attempts to put the parents off the whole idea.

Launch meetings for local CaF groups can range from six parents chatting over coffee in someone's living room to a more ambitious open meeting with a wider audience. For some groups, separated by large distances, first contact has to be made over the telephone or in writing. At the first meeting, a particular issue such as a gap in services may take priority. Attracting more members is often high on the agenda.

A large majority of CaF groups begin by meeting together, comparing notes, sharing experiences and growing together in confidence and stature. They may venture into social activities for both parents and children but never grow much beyond this stage. Identifying common aims and objectives is often more problematic than it looks. It may be assumed that having a child with special needs is a powerful common experience. However, differences among members of a group such as race, ethnic origin, class and age may mean that not everybody feels at ease. It is possible for a group to thrive with a varied membership if there is sufficient common ground and if every effort is made to make people feel welcomed and valued. A good support worker can help this come about.

Recognising the changing needs of a group is vital if the group is to continue to grow. The small home-based group may feel the need to become more structured and form a committee before broadening their interests. Some develop links with other similar groups on a regional or national level. In addition to providing support, information and advice for each other within the group, members take on publicity, fund raising and starting some elementary research. The balance between activities benefiting exclusively the members of a group and other parents with similar problems is delicate. Some groups drift away from their original objectives. Members may become too busy with promoting the group and have less time to give and take support.

The very skills and qualities that produce an ideal founding member can sometimes prevent a group maturing if the founder resists new ideas being introduced by other members or refuses to delegate tasks. Leadership in a self help group is a controversial issue as we shall see below, p.61. Some CaF groups come to a natural end when their members are at a different stage of their experience and the group has served its purpose. Others remain in existence waiting for new members to join. Individuals who are no longer in a group may stay in touch with CaF and receive its newsletter and other material.

From self help group to national organisation

Some self help groups remain small and local while others develop into national specialist organisations. The Breast Care and Mastectomy Association (BCMA) is now a national organisation. In 1994, it celebrated its 21st anniversary and changed its name to Breast Cancer Care. The activities of the organisation, which is funded mainly by the Cancer Relief MacMillan Fund, include: producing publications about breast cancer such as *Every Woman's Guide to Breast Awareness*; organising, training and supporting volunteers who give information and one-to-one support to women with breast cancer; running telephone helplines; setting up drop-in centres for women with breast cancer and their carers; and increasing public awareness through the media about breast cancer.

It all started when Betty Westgate, one of the founder members, was diagnosed with breast cancer in 1968 and suffered from the general ignorance and prejudice around cancer at the time. In 1972 she started researching the cancer education field and found that nothing much was being done to educate the public. Some doctors from the Royal Marsden Hospital were supportive. Westgate read a lot to add to her own experience and developed a talk called 'lumps and bumps'. Many people, keen to know more about cancer and after care, attended meetings up and down the country to hear what she had to say.

In 1974, her local paper in Croydon printed an article based on her talk about breast cancer and asking people to get in touch. The *Daily Telegraph* reproduced the article and the national response was enormous. The need for a national organisation was clear and the Mastectomy Association (MA) was formed. The organisation survived on donations for some years. In 1979 they received their first grant from the DHSS, followed by an additional grant from Cancer Relief in 1980. At that point the MA moved out of Betty's home to an office. It appointed workers, registered as a charity, and developed its small committee into a national council. In short, it made the transition from an initiative relying on volunteers to a national organisation with paid staff. It has since produced guidelines and advice for local self help groups.

Forming an umbrella organisation

Some national organisations formed did not start as self help groups, but were set up to provide support for them. CancerLink is one example. It set out to be a resource to all cancer groups. Its aim was to enable resources to be spread more widely for groups to learn from the experience of others, information on common issues to be shared by all types of cancer group, and training courses to be run locally. It also helps organisations formed around a specific form of cancer to produce more focused information.

CancerLink was set up in 1982 by four people with personal and professional experience of cancer. The organisation began by providing information and support to people with cancer as well as developing work with groups. Its funding comes predominantly from the Cancer Relief MacMillan Fund. Currently, CancerLink offers a cancer information service; training and consultancy; and support to self help groups.

More than 450 groups around the country are in touch with CancerLink and receive the quarterly newsletter *LinkUp*, as well as publications such as *Cancer and Employment*, training, information, tapes with information on cancer in ethnic minority languages and consultancy. All groups are completely independent from CancerLink.

Developing a partnership with statutory services

In 1985, mental health groups in the Derbyshire Dales formed themselves into a federation. Since then they have gained recognition from professionals in the area; they have secured funds, initially from the Mental Health Foundation and more recently from funds held jointly by the local authority and the health authority; they have appointed workers and have co-operated closely with the statutory sector to provide a comprehensive service for people with mental health problems.

Their partners in providing this service are the Community Mental Health Team (CMHT) which includes a psychiatrist, a psychologist, two community psychiatric nurses and two social workers, and which has overall responsibility for providing mental health care for the Derbyshire Dales area. The team was set up in 1983 to move away from traditional medically orientated models towards a multi-disciplinary approach.

While CMHT retains responsibility for therapy, medication and clinical intervention, wherever appropriate patients are put in touch with the Federation's workers who can give them more support at home and introduce them to self-help groups. In other words, members of self help groups and their workers take on the task of normalising patients' lives and reintegrating them into society. Combining professional and non-professional care is thought to make the service more effective and to bring greater benefits to service users.

In addition to collective activities groups organise one-to-one support by providing facilitators to help normalise patients' lives. Often these facilitators help people do the things they used to do before they became ill, or teach them new skills to help them cope with a change in their circumstances such as the death of a spouse.

Their activities include:

- Supporting new members when they join a self-help group.

- Accompanying people on visits to shops, doctors, hospitals, etc. to help them overcome agoraphobia or to help establish new patterns.

- Visiting people at home to combat isolation and encourage them to come out.

- Giving people the opportunity to talk about their feelings and problems.

- Helping people who have been in hospital for a long time learn to handle money, prepare meals, do the housework or other tasks as appropriate.

- Supporting relatives and carers.

The support offered by the groups is appreciated by professionals in the Derbyshire Dales. One of the community psychiatric nurses attached to the team explained how they organise the workload:

> For example, a young woman came out of hospital diagnosed as schizophrenic. I look after her for her medication while the Federation workers help out with company and settling her in her new flat. There is no problem in establishing separate roles for different workers. Frequent communication ensures we all know what is happening.

Finally, in Derbyshire Dales people with mental health problems have a voice through the Federation in planning and delivering mental health services. They participate in a local forum, the Local Planning Group, together with representatives from social services and health services. It is in this forum that policy, planning and delivery of services are discussed.

4. PROBLEMS AND POSSIBILITIES

In this section we identify key issues which represent a challenge to the development of self help groups: rural environments; relationships with professionals; organising in ethnic minority communities; questions of leadership, evaluation and consultation, and - last but not least - the availability of resources. Any attempt to develop public policy must take these issues into account and understand the problems and possibilities they present.

Self help in rural environments

Rural conditions present particular difficulties to anyone wishing to start or join a self help group. Distance between communities and lack of public transport makes it expensive for people to attend meetings. Gossip in small villages stops people from getting together around a stigmatised issue such as mental illness or drinking problems. Barbara Croft started a group 'Drinking to Cope' for women with drinking problems in Derbyshire. She found that women were reluctant to join the group in their own village because they did not want the neighbours to know they had a problem.

Contrary to the legend that rural communities are 'closely knit', many people living in villages are isolated. It is not always possible to find others with the same problem or condition within reach. Organising meetings requires travel and this adds to the costs. Furthermore voluntary organisations in rural areas are less well resourced than in big cities. Many of them rely on one or two people who are consequently over-stretched. The lack of voluntary sector infrastructure means that groups have less access to resources. Support workers are not always available or have to travel long distances to meet the needs of groups. Sarah Clarkson, a development worker with many years' experience of supporting self help groups in Herefordshire, explains:

> Working with self help groups, I could easily spend a third of my time in the car getting to places. This is an

> area of 1600 square miles and 150,000 people, but it can easily take me three quarters of an hour to get to Kington, or if the weather is bad or because of potato picking or caravans in the summer, a whole hour. Then I might have a meeting in Leominster one day and in Ross that afternoon and I will spend three hours in the car out of an eight hour day. Whereas people who work in Coventry might spend ten or 20 minutes between meetings.

Voluntary action in rural communities is still dominated by traditional philanthropic attitudes. It is accepted that some people help others who are less well off or who are in need, which is quite a different approach from mutual aid and self help. People who join self help groups want to find others who are similar to themselves. Nevertheless, some traditional organisations offer opportunities for self help groups. For example, the Women's Institutes are extending their networks to carers in rural areas, to enable isolated carers to get together.

Against all odds, self help groups operate in rural communities and achieve the same goals for their members as in urban settings. People find different ways of organising. For instance, they keep in touch by telephone. Some national specialist self help organisations such as the Eating Disorders Association (see p.58) keep a register of 'contacts' in rural areas, who are willing to be contacted by telephone or letter by others with the same condition.

Some groups give themselves non-stigmatising names and meet in the main town to keep a degree of anonymity. Bringing together people who live in different villages requires some organisation. Support workers have to do outreach work, produce publicity, give out information and organise transport to meetings.

In some rural areas, where it is not possible to set up groups, networks are developed alongside personal contacts and friendships. People draw on previous experience such as being a school governor and use those skills to organise a network of people willing to give support. On the whole, in rural areas things happen on a smaller scale and often require more time. One difference between rural and urban self help groups is the number of people who get together at any given time. As Sarah Clarkson says:

> You get the same problems in rural areas, but they are compounded by the isolation and therefore to get four carers together and for two of them to belly laugh for the first time in years is just amazingly successful.

Sometimes, when there aren't enough people with the same problem to set up a group, individuals are encouraged to join an evening class or a less specific group. For example, a young widow, who asked the local community worker for help in identifying other women of her age in her situation, was put in touch with a women's group. The rest of the members of the group had joined when their children left home, or because they lost their job and needed support.

Five strategies for developing self help groups in rural settings were identified by the Self Help Alliance (SHA) programme (see below, p.73), which included four projects in rural areas. A Rural Research Group, made up of SHA development workers and researchers evaluating the programme, describe the strategies for dealing with the particular difficulties of providing support for self help groups in rural areas:[1]

- Use general and non-stigmatising labels - this is particularly relevant to mental health groups.

- Use fuzzy labels - this helps group different issues with a common element together in order to attract a sufficient number of members. An example of this is a bereavement group that was also able to accommodate other forms of loss such as redundancy.

- Draw on known and acceptable forms of grouping - a problem-focused group may raise suspicion whereas a familiar organisation might be more successful in bringing people together. An example of this is the initiative taken by the Women's Institutes described below.

- Locate activities in towns - this strategy can help attract sufficient number of members as well as helping groups remain inconspicuous.

- Work alongside existing initiatives - this helps overcome the problem of scarce resources which is accentuated in rural areas.

Rural development workers employed by the SHA added further strategies drawn from their experience on the four projects in Bassettlaw, Northampton, Rugby and Hereford (1986-89):

- accept the small size of groups

- develop general interest groups rather than issue specific groups

- try to provide transport

- set up familiar events such as day conferences that provide opportunities for forming self help groups

The Rural Research Group concluded that the self help groups supported by the projects varied from village to village. In some areas self help activities could only cope with a limited set of needs and circumstances. In many rural communities, self help and mutual aid could not be separated from voluntary action, volunteering and other social activities.

The isolation of rural carers is an issue that concerns the Women's Institutes (WI). While WIs are not a typical example of a self help group, they may provide an alternative for carers in rural areas. The National Federation of Women's Institutes (NFWI) carried out a survey of rural carers' needs in 1993.[2] The aims of the survey were: to find out from carers what problems they face; to enable members of the WI to plan ways to help carers; to promote the voice of carers among health and social services providers; and to improve the public's awareness of carers' work.

Eighteen thousand questionnaires were sent to WIs in England and Wales, and members undertook to get responses from people who looked after someone frail, had a disability, or was otherwise unable to provide for all their own personal, health or domestic needs. A report has been published based on the findings from 7,780 returned questionnaires (which represents a 43 per cent rate of return):

> The survey uncovered a group of carers living predominantly in rural areas, many of whom had not previously thought of themselves as carers despite having cared for relatives for a number of years. It threw up detailed information about who the carers are, the sort of changes that caring has brought to their lives, the support that they give to the person they are caring for and the financial implications of being a carer.[3]

The survey identified the carers' needs for support and help (one in three carers has no support or help). NFWI followed up their project on carers in rural areas with a conference in 1994 and the launch of a Charter for Rural Carers.

Relationships with professionals

Collaboration between self help groups and professionals occupies a central theme in the literature of self help because the relationship is both vital and problematic.[4] Self help groups and professionals can help each other to be more effective in meeting the needs of people with health and social problems.

The relationship is problematic because the two groups inhabit very different worlds. Judy Wilson has summarised the differences, which are set out in Fig.1 overleaf.

Figure 1
Two Worlds: Self Help Groups and Professionals

	Self Help Groups	Professionals
Structure	Informal	Formal
Decision Making	Participative	Hierarchical
Main Concern	Mutual support and information	Provision of services
Source of knowledge	Through experience	Through training
Degree of permanence	Uncertain	Long Term
Reward for time	Better coping Satisfaction from being helpful	Pay and status Satisfaction from being helpful
Resources	Volunteer help Members' homes	Paid staff Offices
Degree of integration to structures	Low	High
Language	Everyday	Jargon/shorthand

Source: Wilson, J (1995) *Two Worlds: Self Help Groups and Professionals.*

Wilson set out to identify and describe good practice in relationships between professionals and self help groups. She found that some professionals in both medical and social services highly valued the contribution self help groups could make. She also found obstacles and barriers to good practice. Professionals who failed to establish good relationships with self help groups were constrained by their lack of understanding of three aspects of self help activity: the value of knowledge gained through experience, the groups' campaigning role and the unclear boundaries between the contributions of professionals and self help groups. These constraints could be attributed to the professionals' training, which was based on scientific rather than experiential knowledge, to their tendency to resist change and respond negatively to criticism of services, and to their reluctance to share power with lay people.

Self help groups, for their part, often did not know how to approach professionals. Some groups, Wilson observed, were not organised in a way that enabled them to respond to calls from professionals. Some had insufficient time and energy for this, due to the ill-health or other preoccupations of their members.

Yet professionals and self help groups could benefit from working together, said Wilson, precisely because they had different things to offer and neither could substitute for the other. A self help group could enable its members to share experiences, and to give and receive support; it represented an insider's understanding of a problem or condition. Professionals could not do these things, but could provide expert knowledge and access to services. Self help groups benefited from contact with professionals such as doctors, nurses, health visitors, social workers and health promotion workers by gaining access to specialist information and practical resources, by recruiting new members and by influencing the way the services were delivered.

Professionals likewise benefited from being in touch with self help groups. They received feedback about the services they provided; they helped satisfy their patients' and clients' needs for support by introducing them to a self help group; they could educate the public in matters such as health promotion by giving talks to self help groups and participating in their meetings. (see Fig.2 overleaf.)

Figure 2
Who gains and how, when there are effective working relationships

Who	How
Individuals in difficulty	Option of an additional or alternative source of help
Self help groups	More members Higher self esteem Access to resources
Individual professionals	Complementary form of help available Quality of own service improved
Professional system of care	More help for people in need Prevention of some inappropriate demands Access to users' views

Source: Wilson, J (1995) *Two Worlds: Self Help Groups and Professionals.*

Examples of helpful interaction, identified by Wilson, include the provision of practical resources such as meeting rooms, storage for groups' library of books, access to grants, use of notice boards and provision of speakers at meetings. One indication of a professional's positive attitude to self help was when they responded willingly to requests for practical assistance; however, a sure sign of trust came when they put patients or clients in touch with a group.

Wilson[5] concluded that both groups and professionals sought co-operation rather than partnership. She found this term appropriate because of the differences between the two and their disparate powers. She warned that relationships that were too cosy could carry a risk of co-option and diversion, and pointed to the importance of professionals respecting self help groups' right to self-determination. Support provided with a lightness of touch to enable people to learn and develop skills, was preferable, in her judgement, to direct leadership.

From wider experience it seems that relationships between professionals and self help groups vary enormously depending on the group and on the individual professional. Some groups are set up by a member of the medical profession or a social worker. Some have close links with health or social service providers, but were not set up by them. Others are formed and remain outside the system. Similarly, professionals' attitudes towards self help groups range from hostility to active support.

SANDS: A close relationship with professionals

The experience of SANDS (Stillbirth and Neo-natal Death Society) is an example of a positive collaboration between professionals and self help groups. SANDS has four objectives:

- to develop self help for parents whose baby dies
- to improve professionals' management of pregnancy loss, stillbirth and neonatal death
- to continue to develop a comprehensive information service
- to promote research into pregnancy loss, stillbirth and neonatal death, its causes and effects

A contact name is kept by SANDS for every self help group and given to individuals who wish to join a group. Guidelines and information are produced and given to bereavement support groups. SANDS produces a newsletter in which parents who have lost babies share experiences. Cathy Thorpe, the development worker with SANDS who has a special brief for black and ethnic minority parents, gave this account:

> SANDS is funded by the Department of Health, trusts, companies, individual membership and individual donations. It has been in existence for the last 13 years and has 220 affiliated groups and contacts. SANDS produced guidelines for professionals for the care and

support of parents when there is a miscarriage, stillbirth or neonatal death. The guidelines were warmly welcomed by the Department of Health and doctors and nurses in various hospitals. They were a response to a need felt by many professionals and became part of nurses' induction.

SANDS also produced recommendations for good practice in the disposal of the bodies and remains of babies born before the legal age of viability. In most hospitals the guidelines were received well and put into practice. Sometimes, the resources have not been available to enable the hospital authorities to change their system of disposal of dead babies.

Our success is due to good preparation. The material is researched thoroughly and good practice identified and highlighted. We also lobbied and publicised our actions through our press and parliamentary officer. But mostly, our success is due to the groundwork done by the self help groups. The groups build up contacts locally with hospitals, they provide befrienders and collect people's experiences. They then talk to the people who deliver the service, such as nurses, and help them identify ways to change.

'Tranx' groups: a more troubled relationship

By contrast, groups for women addicted to tranquillisers are at the sharp end of a difficult relationship between patient and doctor. Tranquillisers are prescribed by doctors to help women, and less often men, cope with life, manage the unmanageable and contain their frustrations. But as a result people can become addicted and tend to lose their feelings of self-worth. They become passive consumers of drugs legally prescribed to them by their GP.

Joyce, a member of a 'tranx' group in Bristol, describes her experiences with tranquillisers:

> I was on tranquillisers for 20 years, after spending time at a psychiatric unit. I realised that I wanted to come off them when I read an article in the newspaper about a woman who was on Ativan. I recognised the symptoms she was describing. I spoke to my doctor and he said I should not believe everything I read. It was obvious he wasn't going to help me. The community psychiatric nurse told me about Womankind, a self help project and a tranx group that met there. It took three attempts after getting off the bus to go in. There were five women in the room and I was terrified. I was not used to being with people. But I went and I kept going to the meetings every week. I wouldn't open my mouth at first, just listened.
>
> There was no pressure to come off tranquillisers. The incentive came from seeing other women doing it. We all realised how much time we had lost. The group gave us a feeling of safety. We had to deal with the physical withdrawal symptoms and the suppressed problems. It took me a year to come off tranquillisers.
>
> Then I was ready to go back to my life but not as it was before. Through my involvement with the group I attended training courses in assertiveness and producing publicity for the group. I am now on the management committee of the project. There is no funding for the work we do, but we keep it going. It is my way of paying back a debt for the free help I received.

Members of tranx groups often blame their doctors for giving them tranquillisers in the first place. As a result there is a climate of mistrust of medical professionals in some of the groups. Similarly, there is hostility on the part of some professionals who believe that lay groups may be misinforming people who want to come off tranquillisers. Withdrawal symptoms vary from one person to the other.

Eating Disorders Association: perseverance brings acceptance

Some groups find that if they persevere they are likely to be accepted. A local self help group, the Eating Disorders Group in Norfolk, has noticed gradual improvement in the way they are seen by professionals.

The group began in 1976. From the start its members have been giving talks about the effects of eating disorders, mainly to doctors, psychiatrists and psychiatric nurses. There was very little understanding or interest in the beginning. Gradually, professionals acknowledged the help that a group could provide for individuals. The group has since come to feel that there is more respect for their expertise and their contribution to a body of knowledge. A representative of their association has been co-opted onto the local sub-committee of the Royal College of Psychiatry.

Organising self help in ethnic minority communities

Self help has a distinctive meaning in black and other ethnic minority communities. It tends to have a general rather than specific purpose, encompassing a wide range of voluntary activity. It is closely associated with empowerment and achieving equality in a society where race discrimination is widespread. Veronica Roach, a staff member at the Afro-Caribbean Women's Education Centre in Waltham Forest explains what *they* mean by self help:

> This is an organisation which is about women helping themselves. It is specifically for black women. This is because they need to have their own space. Many women are isolated, they come here and meet others in their own setting away from racism. They get different things out of it; for example, the elderly women's group meets once a week to do crafts of all sorts. Their meeting is also a social event for them.
>
> We run training courses at the centre; literacy, numeracy and computing as well as confidence building. Similar

> courses are run at adult education institutes, but it is not quite the same. Our centre offers a social aspect which the women appreciate. It is informal but it is also supported by paid staff. Our users can become members of the management committee and influence the work of the centre.
>
> We aim to help women take control of their lives, not just get a qualification. Of course learning new skills is important so that they can find a job, but self development is crucial. It leads to empowerment. The job of the paid staff is to ensure the courses are organised and that women are participating. There is no shortage of trainees; some are referred by social services. Self help does not mean people have to do everything by themselves. It is more that they have control over what takes place.

This definition of self help is wider than forming groups around specific issues. Guro Huby worked for one of the Self Help Alliance (SHA) projects (1986-89) and made the following observation about self help in ethnic minority communities:

> One of the (unstated) assumptions underlying the Self Help Alliance Programme seems to be that self help is a visible social entity, namely groups, and that the absence of groups denotes inability to practice self help. Such a definition of self help devalues the strength and independence of people who help themselves through the use of private resource networks and voluntary and statutory organisations and professionals. Groups may not be the appropriate form of self help in all cases and in all settings.[6]

Nevertheless, SHA projects also found self help groups formed around conditions that were specific to ethnic minorities, such as sickle cell anaemia and vitiligo, a disfiguring skin condition that can affect anyone but is more noticeable on people with darker skins.

Many more groups develop in settings such as the church, temple, or sewing class. Often, health and social issues are the focus of these groups.

The Self Help Resource Centre in Manchester (1986-1993) carried out an evaluation[7] of the support they gave to black self help groups. They found that self help groups were important in black communities because people did not have access to information and services. Neither did they get involved in mainstream voluntary organisations, which they saw as predominantly white. What they clearly needed was a chance to get together and discuss issues that mattered to them without fear of disbelief or ridicule.

Many of these groups, they found, were informal and loosely structured. As a result the thread that kept the group together was often broken for periods of time depending on their members' needs. Groups tended to form along ethnic lines and around a number of concerns. For example, it was more common to find a Bengali women's group or a Vietnamese group who got together to discuss all sorts of problems and concerns than an all embracing group formed around a particular condition or issue.

What brings people together is their common background and shared experiences in the UK. For example, a group of Turkish women meet every week at the Neighbourhood Centre in Sydenham to have lunch together, give each other support, do keep fit, raise awareness of women's health issues, organise leisure activities and attend English classes. The group is organised by the Turkish Advisory and Welfare Centre which offers advice and help on a wide range of matters such as housing, welfare benefits, domestic violence, disability problems, counselling, immigration, education and training.

Developing and supporting self help in ethnic minority communities means responding to their needs for generalist workers, on the one hand, while opening up the specialist organisations to minorities, on the other (see below, p.81). Funding such work is difficult because it falls between the established areas for grant giving.

Leadership

The question of leadership in a self help group is controversial. Some groups believe that a leader may take power away from the group members and allow them to become passive recipients of help. This type of leader simply replaces the doctor or social worker by telling the patient or client what to do. The potential for self development vanishes. This type of experience has led members of some groups to dismiss the need for a leader altogether.

In some groups, leadership is practised by one or two members reluctantly because nobody else wants to take responsibility. Tasks such as co-ordinating activities and organising meetings are often left to one or two members who may become tired and resentful. Sometimes, the group falls apart when the active member goes.

A different type of problem occurs when the person who set up the self help group does not want to let go. Founding members are often charismatic individuals who have been able to use their energy and imagination to start something new. They are rarely the sort of person who can sit back and let others take over. This may be harmful to the long term development of their group. Some members may become withdrawn while others get frustrated. When groups need to change there is often conflict leading to a change of leadership.

Some self help groups prefer to do without leaders. They argue that without a leader, the members of the group are more likely to treat each other as equals and to participate equally in the proceedings. Sometimes, groups have leaders without being aware of it: self-appointed unofficial leaders emerge and take action on behalf of the group without the knowledge or the consent of all the members. This can lead to confusion and cause the group to lose control of what goes on. If, instead, a group discusses the nature of leadership it wants and analyses the type of leadership it has, it is more likely to avoid problems and to be able to share out leadership functions among the members.

Tom Douglas in his book *Groupwork Practice*[8] identifies two types of leadership: tasks and emotional functions. Tasks include: initiating; information or opinion seeking; information or opinion giving; clarifying or elaborating; summarising and consensus testing. Emotional functions, which sustain the group, include: encouraging; expressing group feelings; harmonising; compromising; gate-keeping and setting standards.

Sharing both kinds of leadership may reduce conflict and disillusionment. The role of a 'central person' or 'key member' often develops naturally, from being the main point of contact for other members of the group. This form of leadership, based on emotional consensus, is appropriate for groups at an early stage of development. As relationships between members become stronger, they can begin to share leadership functions and responsibilities, giving each other feedback and support, and allocating roles to reflect individual skills and abilities.

However, resentment may arise if tasks are shared between paid workers and unpaid group members. People are usually more willing to offer a service for free if everybody else does the same. If funds are available, groups may be able to resolve this problem by making a small contribution to members who are carrying out certain tasks.

Evaluation

The need for evaluation arises among self help groups for two main reasons. Funders want to know whether they are getting value for money. And groups themselves wish to review their aims and objectives, and find out how effective they have been.

The voluntary sector is becoming familiar with the concept of evaluation. Terms such as 'performance indicators' and 'quality assurance' have become common parlance. The requirement for monitoring and evaluation usually comes to self help groups from agencies supporting them. Increasingly, funding institutions want to know whether services reach the people for whom they are intended and whether they maintain standards. In some cases, performance measurement is part of a contract between a funding authority and a voluntary organisation.

Nottinghamshire Social Services Community Support Unit allocates approximately £3 million annually to more than 500 voluntary organisations including drug and alcohol projects in the community.[9] In 1993, it carried out an exercise to monitor and evaluate the organisations it was funding in order to find out how well the services were being delivered and to identify elements of good practice. The exercise showed, among other things, which organisations were in greatest demand and which particular services were required.

This kind of information can help grant-giving bodies to distribute funds and plan more effectively. However, it can be difficult trying to measure performance across a range of organisations. The Nottinghamshire evaluators found it difficult to compare an Elderly Day Centre providing meals, organising shopping and social activities, befriending sessions and welfare advice, with a Families and Children's project addressing such issues as post-natal depression, financial problems, bereavement and coping with stress.

When evaluation is linked to funding and self help activities are submitted to the judgement of an outsider, it may be perceived as threatening by group members and support workers. Projects are sometimes compared with each other, with a view to redistributing resources. On occasions, evaluation has led to a streamlining of services and reduced funding. In some cases, quantitative rather than qualitative measures are imposed. One result may be that groups come under pressure to increase their membership at the expense of other activities.

Another kind of evaluation is carried out directly by self help support agencies or by individual groups. What do such organisations understand by evaluation? The Thamesdown Evaluation Project, set up by the Home Office and the Allied Dunbar Charitable Trust in 1991, produced the following definition:

> Drawing out or determining the value of a project or piece of work; assessments which allow judgements to be made so that an organisation judges its success and measures its progress. Evaluation provides an overall assessment of the performance of an organisation in meeting its purposes and aims and furthering its values. Evaluation answers questions like: Did the project work properly? Did all the work and money make a difference?[10]

Evaluation studies have so far been focused on four levels: assessing the support provided by a local agency[11]; evaluating a national self help organisation[12]; measuring the effects of a self help group on its members[13]; and evaluating the general usefulness of self help groups.[14]

Self evaluation can be an integral part of a group's activities and provide an opportunity for learning. Members of a self help group can reflect critically on what they are trying to achieve, assess their past performance and identify barriers as well as factors that facilitate progress. Typically, an evaluation addresses three questions:

- What has the group achieved? To answer this question, the group needs to monitor its activities and check them against its aims and objectives. Evaluation is an assessment of what has been achieved against what was intended.
- How effective has the group been in pursuing its aims? To answer this question, the group needs to develop some yardsticks or 'performance indicators' against which its achievements can be measured.
- Was it worth doing? To answer this question, the group needs to find out from its members, including those who have left the group, whether or not their experience in the group helped and supported them in achieving their individual aims. If a group's objectives include making an impact beyond its own

membership, for example by raising awareness among professionals, then it is also necessary to ask these 'outsiders' about how they have been affected by the group's activities.

Evaluation can bring a range of benefits to a self help group, including: clarifying aims and objectives, developing opportunities for discussions about shared values, assessing the value of particular activities, identifying other ways of doing things, highlighting problem areas, reviewing practice and improving group processes. However, judging success or failure is not a straightforward matter. It is common to hear from individual members of a group that the most important outcome was that they made a new friend. This may not have been the aim of the group and if the individual subsequently left, it may be seen as a failure. Yet from the point of view of the individual whose need was satisfied, the group served its purpose. In the current contract culture, groups may need help with evaluation. The Charities Evaluation Services[15] (CES) provides general evaluation services and specific training in self-evaluation. CES was established in 1990 to provide a national evaluation support system for the voluntary sector. Funded by the Home Office, Northern Ireland and Welsh Offices, charitable trusts and corporate funders, CES provides training and advice on self evaluation, information, publications and external evaluation services from its regional offices.

Evaluation is never value free.[16] Wherever it takes place, and whoever is engaged in the process, certain questions should be borne in mind. Whose interests and whose perspectives influence the design of the study? Whose needs are taken into account? Is it enough for the participants to be satisfied with their group? What criteria, if any, should groups satisfy before they are judged a success by others?

Participating in a consultation process

Self help groups are increasingly asked to take part in consultation processes to help identify needs and plan delivery of services. There are major advantages not only for groups but also for service planners and providers, but there are also risks and drawbacks.

Collective experiences of health and social services can give group members a wider understanding of what people need and how their needs can be met, as well as how services can succeed and fail. This can usefully be fed into the planning process. Their contribution is likely to be greater than that of individual service users, as John Simmons, Head of Operations in Derbyshire Social Services, explained:

> The Community Care Act demands that individual service users are involved in the planning of services and in the day to day management of those services and in the care planning activity that is undertaken. It is very easy to say that we will involve people. It is not always easy, though, for an individual living in the community to feel able to be involved when a large bureaucratic organisation turns up on the front door and says, "I would like to involve you in planing the services you are going to receive." I think there is an important role there for self help groups in advocating and supporting that individual, in feeling able to communicate with large organisations such as social services, health authorities and GPs... We can't consult with all 950,000 people in Derbyshire: we cannot meet every individual. Therefore it is important that, through groups ... and umbrella organisations within the county, and national umbrella organisations, we develop representative voices that can play a part in that communications process about evaluating what we are doing now, and also looking to future developments.[17]

Members of self help groups involved in consultation can bring back to the group questions, ideas and policy issues for further discussion. Information about future plans, a deeper understanding of how policy is formed and contacts within the services can be useful to self help groups. For many of them, influencing service provision constitutes a major aim and this is one way of trying to achieve it.

But there are drawbacks. Where one member of a group is chosen, or emerges as a representative, to participate in the consultation exercise, there is usually too much paper work for a single individual to cope with. It may be difficult to represent the views of other members of the group, especially when they differ from those of the representative. Time and energy are required that may be put to better uses. Self help group sessions may have to be dedicated to discussions arising from the demands of consultations and consequently groups may have less time for other activities such as providing mutual support and pursuing the shared interests of the members. Furthermore, there is a risk of co-option. A group may lose its independent frame of mind as it is absorbed into the consultation process.

Aware of the possible difficulties, the Self Help and Carers' Support Unit in Hull produced guidelines for groups, with a view to preparing them for meetings with statutory agencies.[18] They include:

- a check list to ask before attending a meeting such as accessibility of the venue to members of the group

- advice on promoting partnership between groups and professionals

- advice for groups giving their views on reports and consultation documents or taking part in a survey

The guidelines also point out, for example, that individual members can only represent themselves, not the 'rest of the world' and should make this clear; group members don't always think the same and the 'representative' should not 'feel pressured into giving a unified view.' Another danger is that, where only one or two self help groups are consulted, they will distort the picture by promoting their own narrow interests.

Resources

The struggle to find adequate resources features prominently in the lives of most self help groups. They need them to start and to continue their activities, to bridge the gap between where they are and where they want to be. In particular, they require:

Practical help

Often, groups need a small amount of money to publicise their group and attract new members, mail out newsletters, advertise a new group, hire a suitable meeting place, produce some publications, and cover telephone and transport costs. Some groups may need a facilitator to help them with organising their activities. The amount of help they need depends on the members' access to resources, the state of their health and their circumstances.

Training to develop new skills

These include how to run a group, counselling, fund raising and assertiveness - to help individuals develop self confidence and support each other. Some groups seek training in using the media and producing publicity.

Access to expertise and information

Although most groups start with their own collective fund of experience of the condition that brings them together, they want to find out more about it. They seek written material and invite experts to give talks and answer questions.

Assistance with campaigning and access to policy makers

Making its voice heard is not always easy for a self help group. If they don't have the appropriate skills themselves, they need access to people who know how to attract the media, how to speak in public or on the radio and television, how bureaucracies operate so that the group can approach policy makers, and how to be represented on committees to influence planning and delivery of services.

Groups are likely to be more or less effective, and more or less able to sustain their activities, according to their success in securing adequate resources. The quest for resources can be one of the activities group members enjoy, helping to bring them together and giving them a sense of achievement. In other circumstances, it can absorb disproportionate amounts of energy and obliterate activities that are central to the group's concerns. Funds often come with conditions attached, and may be offered or withdrawn according to the interests of others who have their own aims and values, which may or may not coincide with those of the group. Access to new resources, or a crisis induced by a shortage of funds, may radically change a group's agenda and interests. Thus the question of resources is of central importance in the development of public policy towards self help and mutual aid.

5. SUPPORT FOR SELF HELP

Autonomy is the hallmark of self help groups, and this may appear to contradict the need for external support. Paradoxically, their autonomy may depend on receiving appropriate support. Our research suggests that most groups could benefit from some help from outside at some point in their development. Their needs range from having a facilitator who attends meetings and helps organise activities to practical help with specific projects such as advice on how to produce publicity. Whether support is available, and how it is provided, can be of critical importance to self help groups in underpinning and sustaining their ability to work productively. In this section we look at different models of support for self help groups and at the different kinds of agency which provide it.

The support provided for self help groups falls into two broad areas; local generalist and national specialist. Local support is usually provided by a worker based in a local agency such as a Council for Voluntary Service (CVS). This worker is likely to support a wide range of groups. Most local self help support centres produce a directory of groups in their area which they use to raise the profile of self help among professionals and policy makers. They also produce information packs with simple advice on how to start a group, how to produce publicity, how to run training sessions, how to find premises and how to raise funding. In addition to the practical help, development workers become involved with groups to a greater or lesser extent depending on the group's needs.

Resources for local support for self help groups have shrunk in the 1990s. A directory of local agencies offering some form of support to self help groups either through a single worker with a specific brief or through a specific project, published in 1989, listed 78 such initiatives. In the 1990s only nine self help support centres are in operation. Funding has become increasingly scarce and other priorities have attracted local resources.

Support on a national level is provided by specialist organisations, such as CancerLink. Furthermore, the Self Help Centre, based at the

National Council for Voluntary Organisations, has functioned as a national reference point for all self help groups and their support agencies.

Facilitating a group

There are two main reasons why self help groups may need a facilitator. The first is that not everyone who joins a group is confident enough or has the necessary experience to participate. The second is that all groups go through different stages of development and may need support in moving from one to another. Some groups, particularly those whose members have a history of psychiatric problems or whose needs for practical help are urgent, require a facilitator more than others.

The experience of mental health groups is that people with problems such as phobias or low self esteem may not be able to participate in a group without individual support. The facilitator's role is to ensure everyone participates in the discussion and decision making in a way that suits them; that everyone listens to the other members of the group; that everyone has the opportunity to make a contribution, and that all members of a group are valued for what they have to offer. Some of the members may need individual help such as one-to-one counselling from the facilitator before they can participate fully in the group.

Self help groups made up of working class people or women or people from ethnic minority backgrounds need a facilitator for different reasons. They usually bring to the group a variety of concerns and needs in addition to the common concern around which the group is formed. The facilitator has to respond to their needs by helping them gain access to resources and information such as housing and benefits. A trust needs to develop between the members of the group and their facilitator before they can go on to become a support group for each other. The Lamp Self Help Scheme is one example. Based in Leigh, Lancashire and funded through the Self Help Alliance, the Scheme supported a women's group based on a working class estate. This group formed around a shared desire to improve services. Members brought a wide range of concerns to the group, including money problems, dissatisfaction with housing, unemployment, poor diet and stress. Besides attending to women's health issues and helping the women develop their self-confidence, this group saw its purpose as "encouraging a sense of community" and took on campaigning on behalf of the local estate for better housing and welfare services.

Ideally, facilitators go through the experience of being in a self help group, learn new skills through training and develop an understanding of how groups function. They either become paid workers or key members depending on the availability of funds. The trademark of a good facilitator is that s/he allows the group to make its own decisions, passes on to the members any skills they may need, demystifies the system so that the group gains access to services and generally empowers people to take control over their lives and the life of their group. The skills of a facilitator include: ability to listen; warmth; assertiveness; enabling and promotional skills.

Support from professionals

Sometimes health or social workers start up self help groups and take on the role of a group facilitator. Their approach reflects their training which is based on learned rather than experiential knowledge and emphasises the need for structures. This is illustrated by the following account describing a menopause support group set up by health visitors at a general practice used predominantly by middle class people with high mobility, in Crewe, Staffordshire:[1]

> Following enquiries in the practice for advice on menopausal symptoms and with health visitors looking to extend their role into other target groups (than mothers with new babies), it was decided to explore the possibility of establishing a menopause support group with other members of the primary health team. This also coincided with a heightened awareness in the media of hormone replacement therapy and osteoporosis...The group was to

> receive sufficient information so the women participants could make real choices as to how they managed their menopausal years... Another aim was to adopt a positive approach to ageing and the role of older women in our society... An eye-catching display was put in the surgery room, although there had been difficulty obtaining pictures of middle aged women from media sources! Eight names were taken and a further four put on a waiting list. These were sent a personal invitation for the beginning of the course.
>
> The facilitators gave a lot of thought to the structure of the programme and importance was placed on where certain topics came in the course. We chose a small informal common room with coffee making facilities. The group met for eight weeks for an hour on a Friday lunch time with extra time allowed after the session for the group to have time to itself. The course was very clearly focused on the menopause. Information imparted included getting to know our bodies, symptoms, HRT, relaxing and relationships with partners. The sessions were well attended and the group continued to meet at people's homes. There was overall satisfaction among both the members of the group and the professionals who set it up.

The facilitator evidently had clear boundaries. Her role was to get a group together, organise sessions, impart information, encourage discussion and, at the end of the eight weeks, let the group members decide what they wanted to do.

The Self Help Alliance

In 1986, the Department of Health and Social Security initiated a pilot scheme to try out different ways of providing support to self help groups at a local level. The scheme, called the Self Help Alliance, consisted of 18 local projects in different parts of the country. It was managed by a consortium of seven national voluntary organisations. Day-to-day management was carried out by a small team based at the Volunteer Centre UK. A total of £1.6 million was spent on the scheme over the period of three years.

The 18 projects were based in established local voluntary agencies such as CVS. Each project typically employed two full-time workers (one as a development worker and the other as administrative and information worker) although there were some variations. A training programme brought the workers together regularly.

The three-year funding carried with it a clear statement that central government would not continue its support and a hope that local authorities and other bodies would fund those projects that had proved valuable. The local agencies where the projects were based would have preferred five years' funding and took the view that a pump-priming exercise by central government could not work unless much more work was put into building relationships with local funders.

By 1994, none of the 18 projects had survived intact. There is no evidence that this accurately reflected the performance of the projects or the feedback from the self help groups or the conclusions drawn by the project workers about the value of support for self help groups. The main reason for the demise of the projects was that local authority funding had run dry.

A team of researchers from the Tavistock Institute of Human Relations followed closely the work undertaken by the Self Help Alliance projects and evaluated the support they provided for self help groups in a series of five reports.[2]

One of these, *The Nature of Effective Self Help Support in Different Contexts*, lists the different roles played by development workers as facilitator, counsellor, practical organiser, liaison, information and publicity officer, group worker, and even case worker in the social work sense of the term. It observes that the development workers have a preferred style of working with self help groups which can be described as 'facilitating and enabling':

> The philosophy behind this approach is one which believes that groups are to be encouraged to be autonomous and independent, and any involvement by a development worker must respect and promote this. Often this required the development workers to be non-directive and to adopt a 'hands-off' approach in relations with groups.

The researchers recognised that mental health groups required a longer and more intensive period of support.The development workers found that they had to do more one-to-one activity; there was a higher degree of dependency; the worker took on board the group's anxieties and fear of failure; and a considerable amount of stress was created. For these reasons the workers needed specific training and a lighter workload. Groups formed in working class communities tended to be generalist and oriented towards mutual aid and campaigning (perhaps because of the trade union tradition); they too required a relatively high degree of support.

The Nottingham Self Help Team

The Nottingham Self Help Team is a long established local support centre covering the geographical area of the Nottingham Health Authority. It started in 1982 as part of the Council for Voluntary Service. Funding comes mainly from the Nottingham Health Authority. Their aims include the following:

- To provide an information service, primarily about self help groups, but also about appropriate health care information, to self help groups, the public, professional workers and students.
- To respond to requests for help in starting and supporting new self help groups.
- To promote and service a network between self help groups in the Nottingham area.

- To support and encourage groups who wish to pass on their experience, views and knowledge to providers of health, education and social services.

- To provide some services for new and established groups and to link them with services elsewhere.

- To work in partnership with people concerned with professional and pre-professional training, who wish to develop their knowledge about self help groups.[3]

Their role is to be an intermediary, putting groups in touch with service providers and with other groups, and helping them gain access to resources. The philosophy underlying the work of the Team in Nottingham encompasses three principles: helping groups help themselves, promoting self help groups among professionals and helping groups and professionals strengthen their links.

The Nottingham Self help Team has managed to secure sufficient funds to allow them to provide a regular service and to develop new areas of work. Other local self help support centres have had less success in this respect.

The Manchester Self Help Resource Centre

Veronica Marris and Carlene Montoute were development workers at the Manchester Self Help Resource Centre, which was set up in 1986 and closed down in 1993 when funds ran out. The role of the Centre, in their view was "to enable and empower; to show people that they *can* do things":

> Some groups don't need us because they just meet and talk in somebody's house or at the clinic. But if they want to organise an event or publicise themselves it costs money. At the resource centre they can use the photocopier, mail out their publicity, receive advice on how to advertise, etc. We can also help by putting them in touch with other community groups.

> Well women campaigning groups or the Diabetes Group may come to a point where they want to expand and need to contact a national group. DASH (Drug Advice and Support in Hume) is an example of a group that has taken off. (The group decided to register as a voluntary organisation and appoint workers). We advised them on constitutions, funding, premises and employing workers. We are more approachable than the Council. And we are more aware of the problems of dependency than nurses or other professionals who want to set up groups.

Networking: the Doncaster Self Help Forum

An important service that can be provided by a local self help support centre is to get the groups in its area together. Elaine Schofield, the development worker at Doncaster Council for Voluntary Service, describes how a self help forum brought Doncaster groups together.

> Although Doncaster has a diverse and fairly strong self help sector, there was a limited amount of contact between self help groups. The purpose was to provide an opportunity for sharing information, experience and ideas. I also hoped that the event would initiate the development of networks for pursuing common interests, strengthening influence on the statutory sector and mutual support.
>
> The feedback from the afternoon was very positive and the meeting generated a lot of discussion and ideas. Members were pleasantly surprised at how much they had in common with groups they had thought were totally unrelated to their own. For example, the members of the Manic Depressive Fellowship found that the problem of diagnosis also applied to the ME Association and the Tranx Support Group. The majority of groups recommended that there should be regular joint meetings of the Self Help Forum throughout the year with the aim of developing joint activities and sharing information, skills and resources.[4]

National support

The national database, produced and up-dated by *Help for Health Trust*[5] - a resource for the Wessex region that provides information on health issues, hospitals, waiting lists, quality assurance and so on - lists approximately 1,000 national self help and support organisations. Some of them employ a large number of staff and provide a variety of services while others are small. Contact-a-Family (p.41) is an example of a national voluntary organisation with a wide brief to support self help groups of families with children who have any type of disability. There are other national self help organisations that are more specific, such as the Cleft Lip and Palate Association (CLAPA).

Most national self help organisations offer some or all of the following services to their members: information on the specific condition around which they are formed, advice/helpline, newsletter, support to groups, training, and help with general issues such as fundraising and organising meetings.

Body Positive

A charity set up in 1987 to support self help for people affected by HIV and AIDS, Body Positive offers:

- a drop-in centre in London
- information services including a newsletter
- local support groups; their activities include counselling and yoga classes
- telephone helpline
- prisoners' support group
- pen pal group

- hospital visitors
- a group of young people
- a women's group
- a national network of self help groups

Funds for Body Positive come from the Department of Health, a number of London boroughs, health authorities and trusts. In addition to paid staff the organisation receives substantial help from volunteers. While most of the organisation's activities take place in London, it is gradually extending its services to other parts of the country.

Alzheimer's Disease Society

Like many national self help organisations, the Alzheimer's Disease Society supports its local groups by distributing written information and guidelines. Its guidelines for group leaders include a list of tasks and roles for which the group leader will hold overall responsibility and delegate where appropriate:

- to make sure practical and organisational aspects of the group are in order
- to consult with members regularly about their individual expectations
- to offer structure and guidance without being over controlling or possessive
- to ensure newcomers are welcomed into the group
- to make the group a safe place for members to be themselves
- to give everyone the opportunity to speak if they want to

- to be sensitive when someone is in distress
- to make information available e.g. local services
- to 'hold' the group through difficult moments
- to support the members in gaining confidence and becoming involved in the running of the group
- to follow up those who stop attending the group, respecting individual choice not to come
- to develop ways of reviewing the progress and structure of the group and to respond to ideas for change

There is some overlap between services offered to self help groups by their national organisation and by local support centres. For example, both may provide information on fundraising, starting up a group and organising meetings. The emphasis, however, is different. The local support centre will be more specific about local resources and possibilities whereas the national organisation will be more useful on aspects that touch upon the particular condition. Both can be useful to self help groups.

The Endometriosis Society

The experience of the Endometriosis Society raises issues that trouble many national self help organisations. Endometriosis is a disease which is estimated to affect one in ten women in the UK in their reproductive years. It can cause excruciating pain and infertility. Hillary Rowe, the director of the Endometriosis Society explained that local groups are affiliated to the society and act on its behalf under one registered charity number. This, however, can have its problems:

> Some local groups feel they don't need head office guidance and are managing well on their own - it's often perceived as head office imposing regimes and rules for

> which the local group feels it has no need. However, the 'regimes and rules' are there to comply with charity law and protect the trustees and others acting on the society's behalf. Well, as to the future... who can predict? I am sure as the charity grows, the uncomfortable mix of charities being forced to become more professional whilst not losing the caring touch may call for re-adjustment, new structures and an open-minded approach. But the benefits of consolidating and invigorating local groups can be the difference between a bedrock for the charity's future development and a bed of stones.[6]

CancerLink

By contrast, CancerLink offers groups training, information, support and publications without requiring affiliation. Self help groups are independent and can decide to do as they like. They cannot use the name of CancerLink neither can they share the charitable status, but they can make full use of the resources the organisation provides.

Increasingly, self help organisations employ black workers with a specific brief to extend their services to black and ethnic minority communities. CancerLink carried out research into the needs of black people with cancer and developed a programme in response to the needs identified. The programme includes the production of audio tapes with information on cancer and telephone helplines in different languages.

By involving black and ethnic minority people, self help organisations collect a wider range of experiences and identify different ways of coping and new strategies developed in other cultures. They are better equipped to help more people and to represent a diverse membership in their dialogue with service providers.

The Self Help Centre

The Self Help Centre (SHC), was set up in 1986 to act as a reference point for information and ideas on support for self help, to develop networks of self help support workers and to raise the profile of self help groups through organising workshops for professionals. It was first funded by independent trusts and since 1989 by the Department of Health.

SHC is based at the National Council for Voluntary Organisations. It developed as a response to the need for national networks strongly felt by workers and researchers involved in supporting and researching self help groups. It was also considered necessary to link up the Self Help Alliance with other self help support agencies and organisations.

Three national networks were set up in 1986: the local self help support workers' network; the network of national self help organisations and the black workers' network. Annual meetings were organised by SHC in different parts of the country for workers to share their knowledge and concerns about supporting self help groups. Network meetings were attended by up to 100 people. Evaluation of the meetings showed that workers found them a useful way to find out more about self help groups, increase contacts and remain in touch with similar projects in other parts of the country or, in the case of national organisations, in other areas of concern.

In addition to the networks, SHC has run two separate training programmes for self help support workers. The first programme included courses in handling conflict in a self help group, leadership and developing a self help group, as well as a conference entitled "Professionals and self help groups". The second programme included an introduction to working with self help groups for newly appointed workers, and a course in training and tutoring for more advanced workers wishing to pass on their skills to key members of groups. The present author, co-ordinator of SHC 1986-90, explained at the time:

> Some support workers have been members of self help groups, others have a background in community or social work and others still have worked in the health services. They all bring valuable skills and useful experiences. Each group also brings their own training needs. Some have a sound understanding of health and social services, but need to learn more about group work. Others know only too well what it's like to be in a group, but need to expand their contacts and increase their confidence in communicating with other agencies.

An evaluation based on questionnaires completed by both the trainers and the trainees found that "trainees valued the opportunity to meet with others involved in similar work":

> They learned from each other. They shared problems and anxieties which arise from doing innovative work. The style of the trainers was also appreciated. Participation and informality within a clear course structure set the right tone for learning.

A quarterly newsletter, *MASH* (Mutual Aid and Self Help), was published with information about self help support projects, reviews of relevant books and reports, news from self help groups and organisations, and articles on current issues affecting self help groups, such as user involvement in community care.

Changes and restructuring at the National Council for Voluntary Organisations have resulted in ending SHC in its present form. The need remains for a national reference point for the wide range of people and organisations involved in the support of self help groups. Local and regional initiatives are crying out for a co-ordinating body. Furthermore, the need to develop international links is growing. European countries are building their own self help support networks and much could be gained from dialogue with them.

6. SELF HELP IN EUROPE AND NORTH AMERICA

In this section we look first at three European countries where self help has developed similarly to Britain - Germany, Denmark and Belgium - and then at two countries where self help has a different history and significance, Hungary and Spain. We report on the deliberations of a Europe-wide meeting of experts in self help support. Next, we consider briefly how self help activities have developed in the United States.

Europe

In the European Union, it is mainly the northern countries such as Germany, Belgium and Denmark in which self help groups are developing with support agencies, similarly to those in Britain. There are some more experimental and isolated initiatives in southern Europe. In Eastern Europe, following the collapse of communism in the late 1980s, there has been a new wave of voluntary activity, including self help groups around health and social issues. New support structures are developing, for example, the Forum of Polish Foundations,[1] set up to promote and protect voluntary organisations by introducing legislation and fiscal regulations.

Germany

Alf Trojan, a medical sociologist at the University of Hamburg, carried out a survey of 232 members of 65 disease-related groups in 1989.[2] He reported that in Germany, as in many other industrialised countries, the membership of self help groups began to increase in the seventies:

> As far as health is concerned, groups exist for most chronic diseases, handicaps and addictions. There is also a large number of other groups that have an impact on people's psychological and social well being: women's groups, groups for single parents, groups for sexual

> minorities, for the elderly and for many other life-disrupting problems.

His study aimed at evaluating self help groups by measuring the degree to which they achieved their aims and objectives. He came to the conclusion that almost all the people in the research sample had experienced positive changes in important respects.

> To summarise the main points: self help groups have an emancipating effect; they help to free members from burdens of disease, from passiveness, lack of knowledge, unsatisfactory relationships and, most important, from professional and bureaucratic domination.

The wider goals such as changing professionals' attitudes, according to the findings of his study, are less frequently attained.

Jurgen Matzat, a psychologist working with self help groups at the University of Giessen has described the support structures for self help groupwork in Germany:[3] He cites as an example the Federal Association for Help for Disabled People which has 56 organisations bringing together people with disabilities and chronic illnesses.

In addition to specialist organisations there are 'contact and consultation centres' providing support to self help groups in 230 cities or districts in Germany. Self help groups are also sustained by a variety of health and social welfare agencies which do some or all of the following:

- explain the general concept of self help groups
- offer access to established groups
- help new groups get started
- supervise groups in trouble if requested
- collaborate with other professional services

- make contact with politicians and administrators

- function as public relations agents for the self help movement

In an earlier article Matzat named as one of the main reasons for the proliferation of self help groups in Germany the principle of subsidiarity:

> This term, originating from Catholic social ethics, means what individuals, what smaller institutions (like the family) or associations (like charities and voluntary organisations), or what bodies (like municipalities and churches) can do on their own initiative should not be supplanted by any superior level or by the state. Social problems should only be solved on a higher level of institution (e.g. social services of municipalities, regions, or federal administration) if the lower levels (especially families and relatives) are not capable of coping with them. Extensive privileges of independent welfare organisations from public authorities in providing social services also derive from this principle of "subsidiaritat".[4]

Accordingly, the German Non-denominational Welfare Association has nurtured numerous citizen's initiatives and self help groups. But there are other self help groups inspired by different principles, such as those organised along the lines of Alcoholics Anonymous. And there are increasing numbers of small autonomous self help groups operating at a local level and adhering to the principle of mutual aid that can best be described as psycho-therapeutic groups.

Germany has been one of the first European countries to set up a national clearinghouse for self help groups and people interested in them. The German Association for the Support of Self Help Groups was formed in 1982 to help people find a group, to support new groups, to put groups in touch with each other, to encourage professionals through training to work closely with groups, to give information about groups to the media and individuals, to create a positive climate for self help groups and to help set up regional and local clearinghouses.

In 1984 these tasks were passed on to a new National Clearinghouse to Encourage and Support Self help Groups (NAKOS), which provides information, facilitates contact between individuals and local clearinghouses, talks to professionals about self help groups, trains local self help support workers and supports the development of new local clearinghouses.

In the 1980s, before reunification, municipalities in many parts of West Germany earmarked funds in their budgets for self help groups. They either funded groups directly or gave groups access to resource centres. Politicians seemed to understand the value of self help and often endorsed it in their election manifestos. More recently, the efforts of self help supporters, researchers and practitioners have focused on developing an infrastructure for self help groups, with clearing houses and mechanisms for reaching out to individuals and groups in the community.

In 1993 NAKOS published a list of 230 local organisations supporting self help groups in Germany. According to NAKOS director Klaus Balke, in the 1970s there were only 20 such organisations and only 39 were recorded in 1984. Balke is predicting a similar growth in former East Germany. A five-year pilot programme entitled "Support for Social Self Help in Eastern Germany" was launched in December 1991, its aim is to create new clearinghouses which, in turn, will set up and support self help groups. However, financial support remains uncertain.

Only in exceptional cases are the costs of staff and overheads of the clearinghouses met from government funds. Staff are often provided by job creation programmes, hired for one to two years with between 80 and 90 per cent of their salaries paid by the Labour Office. According to NAKOS,[5] more stability in the financial support to clearinghouses would make them better able to meet the needs of self help groups.

Denmark

A 1992 survey[6] of a representative section of the Danish population found that about one in seven adult Danes had at some time considered themselves in need of a self help group; one in five adults knew someone who had participated in a group. The types of concerns that brought people together in groups could be classified into seven categories: grief (30 per cent); family problems (25 per cent); illness (17 per cent); mental suffering (7 per cent); accidents (4 per cent); birth (4 per cent); addiction (3 per cent); and others including unemployment (9 per cent). Women seemed to be more likely to join a self help group than men. Furthermore, single people and people without a strong family or work related network needed groups more than others. Physical illness, with the exception of cancer, was not a large category of self help groups, which may, according to Danish self help support workers, reflect on the quality of health services in Denmark.

Support structures for self help groups include the National Volunteer Centre and a number of local support agencies. The Volunteer Centre grew out of an understanding that there was a need to promote and support volunteering. This role was traditionally performed by the Ministry of Social Affairs, but in the late 1980s after many discussions it was decided that an independent centre would offer a better service.

Self help groups are seen as part of a wider spectrum of activity around volunteering. A three-year experiment, *Network and Volunteer Work* was funded by the Government's Social Development Programme, intending "partly to give more people the possibility of engaging in volunteer work and partly to support volunteer work in general, but ultimately also to test a model and the very idea of volunteer bureaux." Its objectives were to:

- promote community closeness and responsibility for one's own life
- make the wish to help others legitimate

- refresh the memory of 'old neighbourly virtues'
- make social work a 'common thing', something that everybody can relate to
- create networks between people[7]

By 1992, 18 support projects had been established in different parts of the country. The National Volunteer Centre is in close touch with them. It also offers advice and guidance, especially to small and new organisations, loosely organised groupings and initiatives, and it supports the development of networks. It provides information, training and education, evaluation, development work and research, advice on legal matters, fund-raising and consultation.

According to a study of six local projects[8], self help groups find the support they offer to be invaluable. The six projects, which are considered representative, are relatively inexpensive to run, but have to survive in a climate of financial insecurity. The researchers found that local authorities and central government were reluctant to fund them. Politicians and officials showed considerable interest in self help groups, and claimed to believe in preventative work, but were not prepared to commit funds.

Karen Rue, the co-ordinator of a self help support centre which services the whole of Copenhagen, explained that her centre received a grant from the government for three years. After this, she was expected to raise money from industry and from trade unions. Rue and other project workers say this obligation puts undue pressure on them, with adverse repercussions for the groups they support.

The Copenhagen centre services groups of poor, unemployed and depressed people who cannot cope on their own. It offers practical help and a support worker for each group. Individuals wishing to join a group are interviewed by the support worker who explains the tasks and the responsibilities as well as the likely positive outcomes. Anyone who wants to start a new group receives additional help from the support worker. Groups are advertised and when a sufficient number of members has been recruited the groups close. The groups in Copenhagen vary in their particular concerns, but their shared starting point is an absence of any social network and resulting loneliness. Groups tend to form around a life crisis; women's groups often form around low self-esteem and lack of confidence; parents of young squatters get together for mutual support, while mental health groups focus on phobias, anxieties and depression.

In Denmark, as in the UK, there are tensions between self help groups and professionals. Ulla Habermann, director of the Volunteer Centre, identified two opposing views held by professionals.[9] One is that people who cannot cope with their own problems are not capable of running groups. The other view tends to romanticise and see the creation of self help groups by disadvantaged people as 'beautiful'. In Habermann's opinion, neither view is constructive for self help groups, since both help to maintain a distance between the professionals and the groups. A further complication is that self help groups often distrust professionals and refuse to have anything to do with them. Habermann identified three possible roles for professionals: initiator, facilitator and consultant. While she recognises the inherent conflict in this relationship, she argues that by supporting groups professionals can make a contribution towards a more generous and egalitarian society.

Belgium

Trefpunt Zelfhulp (Flemish Self Help Clearing House)[10] supports and provides services to self help groups in the Flemish speaking part of Belgium. It is funded by the Flemish Minister for Welfare and the Family, and provides the following services:

- a directory of self help groups
- information
- a library about lay health matters and welfare issues
- help to people who want to start a new group

The definition of self help groups used by Trefpunt Zelfhulp includes groups formed around personal problems in the areas of health and social welfare, but excludes groups involved in collective action around housing, employment and the environment. In self help groups the emphasis is on individual experiences and personal coping.

In 1994 the number of self help groups in Flanders was approximately 1,200 - one self help group for every 3,100 people. Some are large professionalised organisations which focus on service delivery and lobbying, while others are small local groups where personal contact, sharing of experiences and coping are the most important goals. Increasingly, self help groups in Flanders are recognised by professionals and policy makers. Some professionals are active supporters.

Indeed, Trefpunt Zelfhulp workers report that professionals are beginning to offer self help as a part of their service delivery. They initiate groups around problems they identify and refer people to them. The role of the professional as initiator is welcomed by Trefpunt Zelfhulp, but with caution. They are concerned that professionals should ensure that groups receive continuous support if it is needed, and that groups should not be used as a dumping ground for difficult patients.

Trefpunt Zelfhulp functions both as a local resource for groups and as a national support centre putting groups in touch with each other and maintaining international contacts. For the future it aims to raise the profile of self help groups in order to gain more financial support for them.

Hungary

In Hungary, the activities of the National Institute for Health Promotion include consultation and supervision of self help groups, research, and training for group members. Jozsef Gerevich, who works for the Institute's Drug Programme, has observed that Hungarians had little chance over the forty years prior to 1989 to form voluntary groupings:

> The centralisation of the 1950s smothered all initiatives coming from grass roots level and radically eliminated all support systems dating from the period between the two world wars that were still operating.[11]

Since 1989, self help groups have mushroomed all over Eastern Europe. In Hungary alone, some 30,000 voluntary organisations including 2-3,000 self help groups had registered by 1993. Eastern European countries have shown considerable interest in the self help support structures that have developed in the West. There are, however, some important differences between self help activities on either side of the east-west divide. Zsuzsa Csato, president of the Downs' Syndrome Association in Hungary and a worker at the National Institute for Health Promotion, has observed that in Eastern Europe a self help group is more like a working team:

> What has to be changed outside the group is more important to the participant than what happens within the group. Therefore the self help groups are putting issues such as new laws, new types of care and human rights on the agenda. The groups never remain on the level of just talking with each other, because their social needs are so strong.[12]

In addition, Csato points out, demands for care are at a more basic level in Eastern Europe than in the West and discussions about leadership are more complex; the size of groups varies enormously and members appear more willing to participate fully and take turns in carrying out organisational tasks.

Spain

The Division of Health Promotion of the Barcelona City Health Department has been supporting self help and mutual aid groups since 1987. The end of the Franco regime and the transition to democracy in the mid-1970s gave rise to many community organisations, and by 1987 these included 34 mutual aid groups and a further 46 organisations which housed mutual aid activities.

These groups and organisations provide the opportunity for individuals to share feelings and to exchange information. They also organise social, educational and recreational activities. Many registered associations form around a disability or chronic illness. Having begun their lives as mutual aid groups, they become structured organisations offering services to their membership.

A research project carried out for the Division of Health Promotion in the late 1980s[13] explored the range of self help groups in Barcelona. The project itself was considered to have made a major contribution to the support of self help activities by spreading the idea of self help among professionals and associations of chronically ill and disabled people. Articles on self help were published in professional journals and a video was produced for use in courses and seminars. Mutual aid has since become part of the social workers' course curriculum at the University of Barcelona School of Social Work.

Support is given to individuals wishing to join a self help group and to groups wishing to connect with other groups. Practical help such as finding meeting places, photocopying and getting volunteer help is provided and some financial assistance has been given to help develop groups in the field of AIDS and HIV. A directory of self help groups produced by the Division of Health Promotion shows an increase in both the number and the types of self help groups in Barcelona. Among registered organisations active in the health field, between 1987 and 1991, the number of problem areas rose from 27 to 50 while the number of organisations rose from 46 to 87. Over the same period, among other mutual aid groups identified by health and social work professionals in the city, the number of problem areas covered rose from eight to 20 and the number of organisations rose from 34 to 68.

The expansion of self help activities is partly due to the efforts of the local government, but support workers at the Division of Health Promotion maintain that the development has been largely spontaneous, and that it is not confined to Barcelona. Government bodies in Andalusia and in Madrid have produced directories of self help organisations.

Differences remain between Northern and Southern Europe in the pattern of development of self help. One possible explanation is that notions of individual responsibility and self-reliance are more deeply entrenched in Protestant countries. Another is that in Southern European countries universal access to medical care is a recent achievement and thus subject to less public criticism. Furthermore, extended families and traditional rural societies, which provide their own support structures, are less common in Northern Europe.

Networking in Europe

A European Expert Meeting on Self Help, organised by the Danish Volunteer Centre, took place in Kolding, Denmark, in September 1993. It aimed to strengthen the network of people involved in the support of self help groups in Europe and to share knowledge and information among them. A similar meeting had taken place in Frankfurt in 1991 and in 1992 an international conference on self help in Canada had been attended by European self help support workers. The Kolding meeting focused on four issues: the definition of self help; support for groups; working with professionals; and the conditions for self help in Europe.

The need for a common definition of self help arose from the wish to communicate and share experiences among people supporting self help groups in different countries. It was also considered useful to employ terms which were easily understood by the funding authorities and policy makers. It was not easy, however, to agree on a precise sequence of words. A definition can be either so loose as to be meaningless or so precise as to hamper a group's development. Participants at Kolding came to the conclusion that a distinction needed to be made between the principle of self help and the way it is expressed in practice. The principle of self help is based on one or more citizens taking responsibility for a situation and trying to change it. In practice, this activity is increasingly taking place within organised groups.

Having agreed that groups vary in size, degree of organisation, activities and goals, participants focused their discussions on providing support for self help groups. No-one argued from practical experience that outside support for self help groups could undermine their autonomy. The key question was not whether groups should be supported, but whether there were sufficient resources to do so. Support was usually offered by organisations and projects funded for the purpose, but the amount and the continuity of the support varied widely.

The discussion about working with professionals raised issues around trust and communication. Professionals might support groups in theory, but they took care not to transfer economic resources from their own field of work to a movement dominated by lay people. Could lay people ever convince professionals that they knew what they were doing? It was agreed that, despite the doubts and mistrust, self help groups and professionals had a lot to gain from working together. Information and resources such as rooms for meetings and copying facilities were clearly useful to groups. Professionals could gain insights into conditions that would supplement their knowledge. Sometimes the two could benefit from collaborating over campaigns to improve services.

Participants recognised that it was difficult to 'market' self help activities to the general public. Advertising went against the grain for self help groups, which often thrived in anonymity and under promise of silence. Publicity for self help tended to promote a uniform and formal image which belied the informality and diversity of self help groups. If efforts were to be made to attract public interest it was important to be open about the limitations as well as the achievements of self help. There was general agreement about the importance of expanding and consolidating support and research; secure resources, a steady flow of information and serious analysis were needed to respond to this growing area of activity.

Self help groups in the USA

In 1987, C Everett Koop, MD, Surgeon General of the United States Public Health Service, addressed the plenary session of the Self Help and Public Health Workshop.[14] He explained to the large group of participants, who had come from all over the country, why he thought it was wise to invest the power and prestige of his office in the self help movement.

His experience as a medical practitioner had taught him the importance of self help groups in helping their members deal with problems, stress, hardship and pain. As a paediatric surgeon in the 1940s he had observed that one of the most important ways to help struggling families was to introduce them to one another. He also experienced the benefits of mutual peer support as a doctor coming together with other medical staff to deal with their own grief and stress when children in their care were dying.

Dr. Koop stressed the value of self help groups in helping the medical profession understand more about human behaviour:

> how people interact with each other and their physical environment; how they respond to life-cycle events such as childbirth, family growth, the maturation and departure of the young, and death. We need to understand how people cope with economic, social and cultural stress; how they perceive the future and how they see themselves as part of it. This kind of knowledge tells us not only about health, it tells us about wholeness.

Five years later, one of the recommendations from the workshop materialised in the form of a commercially published book entitled *Self Help Concepts and Applications*.[15] This outlined the contribution that self help groups could make, including: identifying with people who have the same concern; ending isolation; advocacy and educated consumerism; cost-effective mutuality; empowerment; and rethinking the doctor-patient relationship. In the US, as in parts of Europe, the 1970s and 1980s witnessed a mushrooming of autonomous grassroots self help groups, most of them operating with little or no professional involvement. The media helped spread the word about them. The popular TV chat show hostess Oprah Winfrey, for example, made frequent references to the benefits that could be obtained from self help groups.

As the groups flourished and multiplied, the need for structures to support them also became apparent. Centres in the USA, known as 'clearinghouses' provide support for self help groups and put individuals in touch with them. The National Self Help Clearinghouse, for example, was founded in 1976. It encourages and conducts training activities, provides speakers for professional, lay and public policy audiences, sponsors a Women's Self Help Centre, and publishes manuals, training materials and a newsletter, the *Self Help Reporter*.

The New Jersey Clearinghouse, set up in 1981, also functions on a national level and developed in 1990 the American Self Help Clearinghouse. Both are based at St. Clares-Riverside Medical Centre, Denville. They maintain information on clearinghouses, publish the national *Self Help Sourcebook* and distribute mutual aid/self help network computer software and a database for the use of other clearinghouses in the United States and Canada.

In spite of the fact that they are widely recognised and popular, clearinghouses are poorly funded. According to one commentator, policy makers have not yet fully appreciated the contributions they offer in the fields of health and human services.[16]

Relationships with professionals

One of the areas where self help groups focus their attention is collaboration with professionals. Phyllis Silverman, co-director of a child bereavement study at Harvard Medical School's Department of Psychiatry, has observed:[17]

> Many professionals have a very inflated view of their power to help people. They take people in and make them

> their patients or clients and assume that they can provide what is needed. This assumption of expertise can be very inappropriate, especially in the face of the disabilities and human pain represented here.

Having learned from her experience with the Widow to Widow programme, she developed guidelines for professionals working with self help groups, which recognise the limitations of professional knowledge and define a role for them as facilitators or consultants:

- The relationship between consultant and consultee is that of colleagues.
- Consultants must appreciate that groups have value systems of their own by which they judge their own work and whether or not they have achieved their goals.
- The consultant cannot tell the consultee how to integrate into the group's functioning the additional information provided.
- The consultant is a visitor, not a group member, and can take no responsibility to see that suggested ideas are implemented.
- The consultant can be dismissed at any time.

Silverman concluded that one of the important roles professionals could have was that of a linking agent: the consultant's primary task, she said, was to link groups with each other or to provide them with relevant information gathered from groups with whom they had no direct contact. In this way, professionals could endorse the fact that groups learned from each other using experiential rather than professional knowledge.

Computer networking

Computers are increasingly used not only to store data but also to put people in touch with each other. Ed Madara, the director of the New Jersey Clearinghouse, writes:[18]

> On Wednesday and Sunday nights, there are open Alcoholics Anonymous meetings that people from across the country attend on CompuServe. A diabetes group meets Thursday evenings, and the closed incest survivors group is on Friday. Yet those participating in such national meetings never leave their homes. People are using their home computers to go beyond the bounds of traditional face-to-face groups to share common concerns, practical information, emotional support, and advocacy plans via electronic networks and communities.

New computer networks, based on Bulletin Board Systems (BBS), provide mutual help through message exchanges or actual group meetings. BBS makes it possible for an individual to leave messages. Subsequent callers to BBS read these messages and key in their replies. Some BBSs also offer on-line meetings or conferences. For example, teenagers who have parents with chronic illness share their experiences and feelings on a Toronto BBS. An elderly widow wakes at 2.00 am and logs on to SeniorNet to participate in discussions that range from coping with health problems to current events.

According to Madara, people find these meetings neither cold nor impersonal. They make friends, exchange telephone numbers, and worry if someone has not been heard from. With time, says Madara, more affordable computers and integrated communications systems will enable more people to participate in mutual aid efforts and self help communities. Since 1990 the New Jersey Clearinghouse has included a section in its manual on how to participate in mutual help via computer. With international links a new form of community could develop. People could be helped to organise, join networks, educate and advocate to meet their needs.

An unpredictable future

Alf H Katz, a leading US researcher and author on self help groups, noted at the time of the Gulf War, that all over the USA "spouses, parents and other relatives of persons in the armed forces followed classic self help principles in organising to secure better resources for dependents, an equitable allocation of call-ups and risks for service personnel and reserves, and respectful consideration for the consciences of dissenters." He cited this as one example of the dynamic growth of self help initiatives. According to Katz, self help "embodies simultaneously a philosophy, methods that have a common base but vary a good deal, and a vast array of organisations that comprise a major and enduring social force." But Katz warned against trying to encapsulate it in terms that were static and would quickly become obsolete. Self help was constantly evolving and changing, and was likely to develop in unpredictable ways.[19]

CONCLUSIONS AND RECOMMENDATIONS

The idea that individuals with a common problem or concern should get together to help each other is as old as human society. Self help has always been a feature of community-level activity in Western industrialised countries. What has changed is that, in the last two decades, self help has expanded rapidly, gaining new visibility and, arguably, a new political potential.

The self help renaissance

This renaissance of self help in the late 20th century coincides with a time of crisis and reappraisal for post-war welfarism, and with a time of diminishing public confidence in traditional representative democracy. It can be seen as a response to the failure of centralism and paternalism, two powerful tendencies which have helped to shape Western welfare democracies. Yet it also challenges the ideals of neo-liberalism. It involves individuals combining in small groups to provide for each other what the market cannot provide. Self help, as described in this report, is about sharing knowledge, skills and power - the antithesis of a marketplace where the fittest survive and the weakest go to the wall.

Self help has much in common with voluntarism and charity: people doing things for others without prospect of commercial gain and out of a desire to make the world a better place to live in. However, there are essential differences. Self help is not primarily about altruism or philanthropy; it is not about helping others less fortunate than oneself. It is about self-determination and co-operation, and those who are involved are all in the same boat. It can be seen as part of the voluntary sector, but while most traditional voluntary organisations are paternalist, self help groups are, in essence, liberationist. They are about people making their own choices and taking control over their own lives. Our proposals are concerned with self help, not with the voluntary sector in general, which lies beyond the scope of this study.

Remodelling the welfare state

It would be impossible to count the number of self help groups in Britain. In this report we have tried to indicate the enormous range of organisations. They vary widely in their objectives and in their style of operation, but they share distinctive features which we have described. Taken together, they add up to a vast body of activity through which personal and social needs are identified and met. If the principle of 'subsidiarity' can be understood in terms of concentric spheres, with the individual at the centre and the transnational community at the outer rim, then self help, next to family and friends, occupies one of the innermost circles. Those who seek to remodel the welfare state for the 21st century should take this into account.

The Commission on Social Justice, which analysed the requirements for 'national renewal' in its report in 1994[1], sets out four central propositions. The first three are: to transform the welfare state from a safety net in times of trouble to a springboard for economic opportunity; radically to improve access to education and training; and to promote real choices across the life-cycle in the balance of employment, family, education, leisure and retirement. The fourth is perhaps the most relevant to this discussion:

> We must reconstruct the social wealth of our country. Social institutions, from the family to local government, must be nurtured to provide a dependable social environment in which people can lead their lives. Renewal can come from the bottom up as well as from the top down.

Elaborating on its fourth proposition, the Commission observes that however much is done to extend personal independence, "the reality is that we are more and more interdependent":

> It is by what we do together, as well as what we do on our own, that we determine our future. Our quality of life depends on the quality of the communities in which we

> live... we need to build from the bottom up, creating structures of power that release the talents and potential of ordinary people. What central government can do for people is limited, but there is no limit to what people and communities can be enabled to do for themselves.

The Commission acknowledges the primary importance of enabling people and communities to do things for themselves. By implication, tomorrow's welfare system should be developed with this idea - of which self help groups are a significant manifestation - at its core. It would require a radical departure for policy makers and planners. Apart from a brief period of experimentation, which we describe on p.88, self help activities have been consistently ignored by governments since the birth of the welfare state.

The first step would be to acknowledge the existence and scale of self help activities, to recognise that they have a vital and legitimate role in defending and extending the well-being of the people. This recognition would come from national and local government, but it would have to be endorsed by professionals in health and social care. It would mean accepting that problems can be solved from the core outwards, as well as from the periphery inwards. Formal and institutional solutions need not be imposed where families, relatives and communities - through self help groups and other means - are willing and able to invent and manage their own.

Locating self help near the centre would mean conceptualising and organising a welfare system around a body of activity that is by nature unpredictable and unmanageable. If that sounds like a planner's nightmare, it is worth remembering that most dynamic and inventive human activities are inherently disorderly and hard to control: that includes not only what happens in families and among groups of friends and community networks, but also developments in science, technology and commercial enterprise. One need only consider the ways in which global communications are changing to see how the task of planning around uncertainty has become an imperative for policy-makers and governments. Policies that rely upon firm predictions or that are directed towards clearly defined end-states, or that attempt to batten down dynamic social or economic developments are doomed to failure.

To insist that self help is a core activity is not to suggest that we load new responsibilities upon it by cutting back state services and leaving people to fend for themselves. Nor is acknowledging that it cannot be measured or controlled a call for government to retreat and for anarchy to reign. The point is to recognise both the strengths and the limitations of self help, and to understand what it can and cannot achieve. We can then consider how best to sustain self help activities, what changes, if any, would have to be made to this end within statutory services, and what can be done at the interface between the two, to ensure that relations are co-operative and productive.

Value and limitations of self help

As this report demonstrates, self help can be valuable at a number of different levels. For individuals it can put an end to social isolation, helping them make friends and join groups of people with whom they have something in common. It provides individuals with access to psychological and social support as well as practical advice and help - with conditions ranging from physical illness and disability to mental disorder and addiction, from housing and debt to violence and sexual abuse, and from racism and sexism to caring for dependent relatives. Groups which do not address problems, but are concerned with shared activities (sports, leisure, arts, etc) can be included in a broad definition of self help, being self determining, co-operative, and committed to mutual support to meet members' needs.

Self help groups of all kinds invigorate civil society. They can be an important source and conduit of information and experience: knowledge which is circulated among members and transmitted to planners and service providers. They provide one means by which the voices and views of ordinary people can be heard in consultations with government bodies. They can raise awareness about particular problems or conditions, pressing for changes in public opinion and in public policy. Sometimes groups themselves act as service providers, occasionally under contract to statutory agencies, but more often informally by providing their members with a service which is delivered inadequately or not at all by the state. More generally, self help activity is rather like a good compost: it helps to construct and invigorate social networks and communities. And, as the Social Justice Commission points out, building the health and strength of local communities is a key strategy for national renewal.

Self help activity is unevenly distributed across the country, as well as between social classes and communities. It is fragmented and often transient, as groups spring to life and die away of their own accord. In the main, groups are small, localised and tend to introspection. Many have a narrow perspective, focusing on a single issue. They are fuelled by human resources - time, energy and empathy as well as practical skills - whose flow cannot be anticipated with any certainty, and which individuals possess in widely different measures. Self help groups sometimes distribute information beyond their own ranks, but when they provide services other than purely informational ones, these are only for their own members; the range of services they are able to provide depends on the variable capacities of their members. Self help scores high on inventiveness and diversity, and low on equity and consistency. Clearly self help groups cannot provide health and social services to the public at large. Even for their own members, they are neither competent nor willing, nor expected to provide most essential services.

However, the fact that conventional service delivery is a marginal activity for self help groups should not consign them to the margins of a 21st century welfare system. Just as self help groups are far more than second-rate service providers, so the health and wellbeing of the population depends on far more than conventional service delivery. Next to poverty, unemployment and homelessness, major determinants of ill health are social isolation, stress, ignorance and a sense of powerlessness; these are among the main reasons why individuals are unable to make choices, to participate in society and realise their full human potential. Self help groups cannot be expected to combat all of these factors, but most of them will help to combat some. If the value of this contribution is appreciated, the next step is to find ways of spreading self help opportunities as widely and as evenly as possible.

Public support for self help

Public policy cannot force people to form or join self help groups, but it can create the conditions for all kinds of self help activity to flourish in all kinds of community. A priority, then, for tomorrow's welfare system is to encourage self help and facilitate greater equity of access by funding a range of designated local and national support operations. It has been argued in the past that any kind of organised support for self help would constrict or distort the activities of groups, destroying their authenticity as independent and anarchic formations. However, there is no evidence to support this view. Our findings in general and particularly the experience of the Self Help Alliance indicate that initiatives to support self help can make a significant impact, enabling groups to form, to survive, to grow and to be effective in their own terms, without threatening their freedom or undermining their identity. We are not proposing that self help groups be funded directly, but that funds be committed to local organisations which support self help groups. There would be no obligation, obviously, for groups to accept support; many would neither need nor wish to do so.

Support can be especially helpful for groups in disadvantaged areas where indigenous resources are scarce and where problems are likely to be more generalised as well as more serious. It is increasingly necessary as groups are expected to participate in more and more consultative exercises: without support, our research suggests, many are in danger of buckling under the weight of demands to take part in surveys and meetings, and to read and comment on reports and proposals. So public support for self help groups is a *quid pro quo* for their role in participatory decision-making.

As we have shown, a range of models for self help support is available. Different strategies are needed for different conditions and purposes. What is required to stimulate and sustain self help activities in a rural area is unlikely to be the same as for an urban setting; poor and ethnic minority communities may need a different kind of support from that required by groups brought together by a shared illness or disability. Support may be offered horizontally across localities, or vertically from national organisations to local groups. Both kinds are valuable. While the former is usually general in character and available to all kinds of group, the latter tends to be specialist, linking a national umbrella organisation with local groups.

Key functions of self help support

Support to groups would be largely 'in kind' and would include shared resources for copying, printing and meeting rooms, information, training, publicity, opportunities for networking with other groups and with professionals, outreach to particular communities and groups where there are no established links, facilitators to help start up and run groups, and research both into particular conditions and into the methods and efficacy of self help. The purpose is to enable groups to meet their own goals; groups should remain free to do as they like, but with the opportunity to use the resources offered by the support organisation, with an absolute minimum of conditions attached.

In addition to enabling self help groups to form, flourish and achieve their own goals, support organisations would have an important role to play in:

- mapping the extent of self help activities in the locality, providing a comprehensive database and making it widely available, enabling individuals to contact groups, and groups to network with each other and with specialist umbrella organisations;

- providing a channel for local groups to participate in consultative exercises with elected representatives and statutory agencies, so that their experience and views contribute to the political decision-making process;

- promoting mutual understanding and productive co-operation between self help groups and local professionals in health and social care, as well as other local government officials;

- helping to develop criteria by which the effectiveness both of self help support and of self help activities in general can be assessed.

Possible funding mechanisms

Support for self help is relatively inexpensive. The Self Help Alliance, which comprised 18 new, local projects to support self help, cost £1.6 million over three years from 1986. At today's prices, to support a larger number of projects spread across the country, we estimate a cost of between £6 million and £9 million a year. By comparison, a single local authority spends some £75 million a year on social services and a typical annual budget for one district health authority is £300 million.

The experience of projects funded through the Self Help Alliance demonstrates the failure of short-term financing. Projects were unable, by and large, to find alternative sources of funds and had to close down after three years. Financial support from government should be a clear and sustained commitment. Funds would be drawn from central government (chiefly from the Department of Health, but possibly also from the Home Office as well as the Scottish and Welsh Offices). They could be administered at a national level by the Department of Health, aided by advisers with suitable expertise in self help. One possible mechanism for administering funds at a local level would be the Joint Consultative Committees which currently distribute funds ('joint finance') for projects outside the NHS which are intended to improve the health of the local population. However, the present joint financing arrangements are time-limited: careful preliminary planning as well as more flexibility, allowing for continuous funding in appropriate cases, would be needed to sustain self help support.

Public funds would be for local and horizontal forms of support. Specialist national umbrella organisations, supplying vertical support, would continue as at present to finance themselves through their own national and local fund-raising, by applying to charitable foundations and by seeking grants directly from central government departments (most obviously the Department of Health). These arrangements should be subject to periodic review to check that national umbrella organisations continue to be able to sustain themselves in this way.

The aim is not to set up identical support agencies in every locality, but to 'grow' them from fairly modest beginnings, on a gradual and experimental basis, so that a range of models can develop to suit different needs and expectations. Local organisations could be invited to apply for funds to develop self help support. Possible candidates include Councils for Voluntary Service, Rural Community Councils, Volunteer Bureaux, Citizens' Advice Bureaux, Community Health Councils, community development agencies and Settlements, such as Oxford House in Bethnal Green, East London. Only one grant should be awarded in each area, so that resources are not spread too thinly, although this need not be a hard and fast rule.

Conditions attached to the grant would vary according to local circumstances, but arguably within a common framework determined at a national level. This might include a very broad definition of what constitutes a self help group eligible for support, and guidelines for ensuring impartiality and guarding against abuse. We have already outlined a range of functions that can be performed by self help support organisations. Chiefly, support would be in kind, although it would be open for support organisations to distribute small ad-hoc grants of up to, say, £300 to local groups on an occasional basis to support particular activities. The balance of support functions would vary from one locality to another, and would vary over time. Support organisations could be encouraged to seek additional funding from other sources, but should not have to rely on this for survival.

One or more national organisations could be supported (building perhaps on the Self Help Centre at the National Council for Voluntary Services) to link and develop self help support organisations. They could help to train support workers, build networks between them, contribute to quality assurance programmes, keep in touch with developments overseas, promote self help and appropriate research, and represent local support organisations at a national policy-making level.

Quality assurance

Wherever public funds are spent it is necessary to find ways of rendering the recipient accountable and measuring whether the money is being put to good use in the public interest. Where a support organisation gives a small grant to a group it would be reasonable to expect the group to account for how the money is spent and for some assessment to be made of the outcome. Except in these circumstances, however, it would be futile and even counter-productive to subject self help groups to any systematic quality assurance, or to attempt to make them account for themselves.

The performance of support organisations, on the other hand, can and should be evaluated. Self help groups and the support organisations themselves should be involved in defining objectives and standards, and local groups should play a part in monitoring the performance of their support organisation. The grant held by the support organisation would be for a fixed term (say, five years). Renewal would depend on a positive evaluation; if it failed, the grant could be awarded to another organisation.

In addition, a programme of more detailed, longitudinal research should be undertaken, possibly funded through the ESRC, to analyse the development of self help activities, to help assess their impact on individuals and communities, and to examine the implications for the statutory services. The government's strategy for investing public funds in self help support would be reviewed periodically, taking account of local evaluations and research findings as they become available. As with local assessments, criteria should be developed in consultation with local self help groups, as well as with professionals in health and social care and others with relevant knowledge and experience. The aim should be to assess not only the scale of activities, in terms of how many groups have developed over time, but also how individual group members perceive the effect upon themselves of involvement in self help and how these findings correlate with indicators of the health and wellbeing - in the broadest sense - of the local community.

Relations with professionals, politicians and government officials

A welfare system which recognises self help as a core activity will require a profound and widespread change of attitudes. If individuals are to be enabled to make their own choices and take co-operative action to help themselves, then power cannot be monopolised by 'experts' who believe they always know best. Professionals in health and social care, as well as politicians and government officials, will have to learn respect for individual citizens and for self help activities. Self help support organisations can be essential in helping to break down barriers, facilitate dialogue and educate professionals and others about self help. Learning from and liaising with self help groups should become an integral part of professional training programmes. Professionals can contribute by acting as catalysts and supporting the start of new groups, by referring individuals to them, and by sharing knowledge. We suggest that they should also accept that some resources be diverted from their own services to fund support for self help. A strong lead from government would be necessary to bring professional bodies into line with the policy. The point is not that self help groups should usurp the role of the professionals, but that both would benefit from closer co-operation. As we point out in the report, the goal should be to build mutual confidence and understanding between self help groups and professionals.

Relations with the voluntary sector

Self help has an uneasy but often fruitful relationship with the rest of the voluntary sector. As we have stressed, self help is quite distinct from voluntarism or charity; it offers a critique of the paternalist conventions of many voluntary organisations. Yet the ethos of self help has permeated many of them, changing their goals and their practices. Some voluntary organisations have managed to combine philanthropic activities and service delivery with efforts to develop and support local self help groups. Others regard self help groups with fear or disdain. A national strategy for self help could usefully be combined with a strategy for the voluntary sector (beyond the scope of this study) which acknowledges the differences and seeks to build a productive relationship between them. The NCVO could have a key role to play in this development.

Summary of recommendations

- Public policy should acknowledge the scope and scale of self help activities and the contribution they can make, directly and indirectly, to the health and well-being of the population, and to the vitality of civil society.

- A remodelled welfare system for the 21st century should recognise self help as a core activity. That implies understanding its strengths and limitations, organising support systems around it, and changing the ethos as well as some of the practices of the statutory services.

- The aim should be to create the conditions for all kinds of self help activity to flourish in all kinds of community; to spread opportunities for self help widely and as evenly as possible.

- To this end, public funds should be invested in local organisations which offer support to self help groups. Funding would be relatively modest but should be on a continuing basis, to be distributed by the Department of Health and possibly administered through Joint Consultative Committees. It is envisaged that one support organisation would be set up in each locality, and that a range of local organisations could be invited to apply for the grant.

- Self help support should be encouraged to develop gradually and experimentally, using a range of models to suit different conditions.

- One or more national umbrella organisations for self help support should be publicly funded to provide training, networking opportunities, and liaison with self help overseas, as well as with policy makers and opinion formers.

- Self help groups cannot be subject to quality control, but self help support organisations should be monitored and evaluated.

- Longitudinal research should be commissioned to explore the effects of self help on individuals and communities.

- Public investment in self help support should be kept under review, taking account of the evaluation of support organisations and long-term research findings.

- Criteria for monitoring performance of self help support should be developed in consultation with self help groups, professionals in health and social care and others with relevant experience.

- The central role of self help should be reflected in training programmes for professionals and local government officials. If self help is to flourish at the heart of a 21st century welfare state, then the 'experts' must respect the autonomy and capabilities of self help groups.

- A new strategy for the voluntary sector should be developed alongside a strategy for self help. This must recognise the essential differences between self help groups and most voluntary organisations, and seek to build a constructive relationship between the two.

APPENDIX

The research

This report is based on research carried out in two stages, in 1990 and in 1993-94, both funded by the Joseph Rowntree Foundation. The first stage included carrying out interviews with major self help organisations and professionals in the statutory sector and a seminar, which took place at IPPR and involved the key people active in the support of self help groups.

It was clear from the early findings that more research was necessary in order to do justice to such a complex area of work. Furthermore, there was a need for a publication that covered the wide range of self help groups and described more fully their activities. The second stage of the research involved more interviews and a systematic analysis of the nature of self help groups, their problems and possibilities, and their needs in order to formulate policies that can help them thrive.

The self help groups and organisations approached within the context of this research were selected to provide a wide range of examples and to illustrate the key issues in this field of work. A list of them is given below:

National organisations

Alcoholics Anonymous
Alzheimer's Disease Society
Black Volunteering
Breast Cancer Care
British Council of Organisations of Disabled People
British Diabetic Association
CancerLink
Carers' National Association
Centre for Training and Research in Self Care - Holland
Contact-a-Family

Depressives Anonymous
Disability Alliance
Eating Disorders Association
Federation of Community Work Training Groups
Grandparents' Federation
Long-term Medical Conditions Alliance
ME Action
MIND
National Federation of Women's Institutes
People First
SANDS - Stillbirth and Neo-natal Death Society
Self Help Centre - National Council for Voluntary Organisations
Tenant Participation Advisory Service for England
Terence Higgins Trust
Values into Action
Volunteer Centre UK

Local groups and agencies

Afro-Caribbean Women's Education Centre - Walthamstow
Birmingham Credit Union Development Agency Ltd
Black Carers Support Group - Birmingham
Body Positive - London
Child Abuse Studies Unit - University of North London
Citizen Advocacy Project - Plymouth
Derbyshire Centre for Integrated Living
Derbyshire Coalition of Disabled People
Derbyshire Dales Federation of Mental Health Support Groups
Diabetes Self Help Groups - Nottingham
East London Cancer Support Group
Everyman Centre - Brixton
Greater London Association of Community Health Councils
Homeless Network - London
Loughborough University - Centre for Research in Social Policy
Lower Clapton Health Centre - Hackney
Manchester Self Help Resource Centre
Positively Women - London
Rotten Park Winson Green Credit Union Ltd - Birmingham

Self Help Team - Nottingham
Southall Black Sisters - West London
Turkish Advisory and Welfare Centre - Sydenham
Womankind - Bristol
Women's Aid - London

REFERENCES

Introduction

1. There is also a very lively and well organised self help movement in Australia. For a brief description see **Wilson J** (1987) 'Self Help Speaks Out'. *New Society* 13.2.87.

1. What is Self Help?

1. **Smiles S** (1958) *Self Help: with Illustrations of Character. Conduct and Perseverance.* Centenary Edition. John Murray, London.

   Kropotkin P (1972) *Mutual Aid.* Allen Lane, Harmondsworth.

   Both publications are quoted in:

   Vincent J (1985) *Constraints on the Stability and Longevity of Self Help Groups in the Field of Health Care.* Centre for Research in Social Policy.

2. **Havel V** (1991) *Summer Meditations*

3. **Matzat J** (1993) 'Away with the experts? Self help groupwork in Germany'. *Groupwork* Vol.6 (1) pp 30-42.

2. What can Self Help Achieve?

1. **Dibben M** (1993) 'Credit where it's due'. *Search* 17.9.93.

2. **Kelleher D** (1990) *Patients Learning from Each Other: Self Help Groups for People with Diabetes.* Presented at Forum on Medical Communication 1.6.90

3. Scope and Development of Self Help Activities

1. For more information on self help and housing please contact the following organisations:

The Housing Corporation, Waverley House, Noel Street, London WIV 3PB - provides a list of housing co-operatives.

Tenant Participation Advisory Service, 48 The Crescent Salford M5 4NY - provides advice, support, information, training and help to promote tenant participation.

Walter Seagul Trust, 57 Chalton Street London NW1 1HU - gives advice and help on self build houses.

Community Self Build Agency, Unit 26 Finsbury Centre 40 Bowling Green Lane EC1R 0NE.

Community Architecture Resources Centre, RIBA 66 Portland Place London W1N 4AD.

Homeless Network Alliance House 12 Caxton Street London SW1.

2. Help for Heath Trust, Highcroft Cottage, Romsey Road, Winchester, Hampshire S022 SDH.

3. **Morris J** (1992) *Disabled Lives*. BBC Education.

4. **Morris J** (1993) *Independent Lives - Community care and disabled people*. MacMillan.

5. **Anderson C T** (1990) 'Doctors in AA'. *American Medical News* 12.1.90.

6. **Lloyd G** (1993) 'Alcoholic doctors can recover'. *British Medical Journal* 17.3.93.

7. **Gay P** (1989) *Getting Together: A study of self help groups for drug users' families.* Policy Studies Institute.

8. **Nelles B** (1988) 'Groups for HIV positive drug users'. *DRUGLINK,* September/October.

9. **Baker B** (1992) *Taking the lid off ... An investigative report on services in Nottinghamshire for people dependent on tranquillisers.* May.

10. **Fielding N** (1990) 'Black Carers'. *Community Care* 11.1.90.

11. **Tuckman B W** 'Developmental sequences in small groups'. *Psychological Bulletin* No. 63 p 384-9.

4. Problems and Possibilities

1. **The Tavistock Institute of Human Relations** (1988) *Self Help in Rural Areas. Is It Different?* COVAS Occasional Paper no.2 September.

2. **National Federation of Women's Institutes** (1994) *Caring for Rural Carers.* PhD Research Ltd.

3. **Addison-Child I** (1994) 'Caring for Rural Carers'. *MASH* no.31, Spring.

4. **Unell J, Wilson J and Marsden K** (eds) (1992) *Self Help Groups and Professionals. An annotated bibliography of literature published in the United Kingdom between 1982 - 1991.* The Self Help Team, Nottingham.

5. **Wilson J** (1995) *Two Worlds: Self help groups and professionals.* Ventura Press.

6. **The Tavistock Institute of Human Relations** (1989) *Self Help Support and Black People.* COVAS Occasional Paper no.4, March.

7. **Agbalaya F** (1993) *Black people and Self Help.* Manchester Self Help Resource Centre.

8. **Douglas T** (1976) *Groupwork Practice.* Tavistock/Routledge.

9. **Williams G** (1993) *Broadening the Scope for Performance Monitoring in the Voluntary Sector: the Nottinghamshire Experience.*

10. **Thamesdown Evaluation Project** (1991) *An Evaluation Glossary or "Don't get worried by words".*

11. **Unell J** (1986) *Help for Self Help - A study of a local support centre.* Bedford Square Press.

12. **Hatch S. and Hinton T** (1986) *Self Help in Practice: A Study of Contact-a-Family, Community Work and Family Support.* Policy Studies Institute.

13. **Bateman J** (1989) *An Evaluation of the Dartford Agoraphobia Group.* Dartford Community Health Team, Spring.

14. **Richardson A & Goodman M** (1983) *Self Help and Social Care Mutual Aid Organisations in Practice.* Policy Studies Institute.

15. Charities Evaluation Services, 1 Motley Ave, Christina St. London EC2A 4SU.

16. **Pfeffer N & Coote A** (1992) *Is Quality Good for You? a critical review of quality assurance in welfare services.* IPPR.

17. *Care in the Community - The Self Help Option,* Report on the Derby Self Help Conference 4.6.93, published by Derby CVS Self Help, 4 Charnwood Street, Derby 2GT.

18. *Sharing Ideas and Experiences with Health, Social Services and Other Agencies* - Guidelines for self help groups compiled by representatives from groups in Hull 1993.

5. Support for Self Help

1. **Granville G** (1990) 'Facilitating a menopause support group'. *Health Visitor,* March.

2. The reports are:

   1988 Survey of Self Help Support Projects
   Self Help in Rural Areas - Is It Different?
   The Nature of Effective Self Help Support in Different Contexts
   Self Help Support and Black People
   Mental Health and Self Help Support
   COVAS Occasional Papers The Tavistock Institute of Human Relations 1988-1990.

3. **The Self Help Team** (1993) *A Report on the Work of the Team.* October.

4. **Schofield E** (1993) 'Doncaster Self Help Forum'. *MASH* No. 28, Summer.

5. Help for Health Trust, Highcroft Cottage, Romsey Road, Winchester Hampshire SO22 5DH.

6. **Rowe H** (1993) 'Local groups: bedrock or bed of stones?' *MASH* no.30, Winter 1993-94.

6. Self help in Europe and North America

1. Note written by Piotr Konczewski, Chairman of Forum of Polish Foundations distributed at the European Expert Meeting on Self Help, Denmark, September 1993.

2. **Trojan A** (1989) 'Benefits of self help groups: a survey of 232 members from 65 disease-related groups'. *Soc. Sci. Med.* Vol. 29 No. 2 pp 225-232.

3. **Matzat J** (1993) 'Away with the experts? Self help groupwork in Germany'. *Groupwork* Vol.6 (1) pp30-42.

4. **Matzat J** (1989) 'Some remarks on West Germany's health and welfare system and the position of self help', in **Humble S & Unell J** (eds.) (1989) *Self help in health and social welfare: England and West Germany.* Routledge.

5. **Balke K** (1993) *Current and future challenges for self help clearing houses in Germany.* Paper presented to the European Expert Meeting on Self Help, Denmark, September 1993.

6. **Mehlbye J & Christoffersen M N** (1992) *Self Help Groups - Prevalence, Character and Experience in a National and International Perspective.* Copenhagen.

7. **Habermann U** (1993) *Folkelighed og frivilligt arbejde.* Academisk Foring Kobenhavn, p.205. English summary.

8. **Diemer A & Stenbak E** (1992) *Self Help Groups. A Study of Six Danish Self Help Projects.* Copenhagen.

9. **Habermann U** (1990) 'Self help groups: a minefield for professionals'. *Groupwork* Vol. 3(3) pp 221-223.

10. **Gielen P** (1994) 'Self Help in Flanders'. *MASH* No.31, Spring.

11. **Gerevich J** (1989) 'Self help in Hungary'. *Health Promotion* Vol.4 No. 4, pp 272-273.

12. **Csato Z** (1993) *The difference between self help in Eastern and Western Europe.* Paper presented to the European Expert Meeting on Self Help, Denmark, September 1993.

13. **Villalbi J R & Roca F** (1992) 'Supporting and monitoring mutual aid groups and organisations in Barcelona'. *Health Promotion International,* OUP. Vol.7 no.4 pp 283-288.

14. **US Department of Health and Human Services** (1987) *The Surgeon General Workshop on Self Help and Public Health.*

15. **Katz A, Hedrick H, Isenberg H, Thompson L, Goodrich T & Kutcher A** (Eds.) (1992) *Self Help; Concepts and Applications*. The Charles Press.

16. **Wollert R W** (1987) *'A Survey of Self Help Clearinghouses in North America: A Special Report for the US Surgeon General's Workshop on Self Help and Public Health'.*

17. **Silverman P R** 'Critical Aspects of the Mutual Help Experience'. in *Self Help Concepts and Applications* op.cit. p76.

18. **Madara E** 'Tapping Mutual Aid Self Help Opportunities on-Line'. Leaflet available from American Self Help Clearinghouse, St.Clares-Riverside Medical Center, Denville, N.J. 07834.

19. **Katz A H** 'Afterword'. in *Self Help Concepts and Applications* op.cit. pp. 298-300.

Conclusions and Recommendations

1. **Commission on Social Justice** (1994) *Social Justice Strategies for National Renewal.* Vintage. pp.20-22.

What Next? Agencies, Departments and the Civil Service
Anne Davies & John Willman
Aug 1991 ● ISBN 1 872452 40 X
£10

Considers the constitutional implications of devolving Government functions to Agencies, and the issues facing the civil service as it divides more sharply into service delivery and policy work.

Strangers and Citizens: A positive approach to migrants and refugees
Edited by Sarah Spencer
March 1994 ● ISBN 1 85489 051 4
£14.95 (Rivers Oram Press)

A team of specialists in geography, economics, law and social policy analyses British immigration, refugee and citizenship policies and recommends a more informed and principled approach which would meet the UK's international human rights obligations, reflect the economic demand for selective immigration and improve race relations.

The Welfare of Citizens: Developing New Social Rights
Edited by Anna Coote
June 1992 ● ISBN 1 854890 38 7
£9.95

Argues that citizenship in a modern democracy must embody social and economic as well as civil and political rights. Papers by Raymond Plant, Norman Lewis, Wendy Thomson and others include proposals for a charter of social rights; rules for procedural fairness; a role for locally negotiated service contracts and a new approach to the development of children's rights.